Dreams

Hi Betti,
Mich begeistert dieses
Buch total, auch wenn
es für "Australische"
Träume geschrieben
ist, aber ich find' es
einfach toll, wenn man
morgens im Bett seine
Träume "deuten" kann.
Also viel Spass dabei
wünscht dir mit einem
dicken Kuss
Deine
Annette

Dreams
Signs of
Things to Come

Triple J's
Quentin Watts
with
Vicki Canisius

an
ABC
BOOK

Published by ABC Books for the
AUSTRALIAN BROADCASTING CORPORATION
GPO Box 9994, Sydney NSW 2001

First published June 1994
Reprinted September 1994
Reprinted January 1995
Reprinted February 1997

National Library of Australia
Cataloguing in Publication entry
Watts, Quentin.
    Dreams.
    ISBN 0 7333 0152 5.

    1. Dreams. 2. Dream interpretation. I. Canisius, Vicki. II.
Australian Broadcasting Corporation. III. Title.

154.63

Cover photography Steve Bush
Cover illustration Luke Sandstrum
Edited by Jill Wayment
Designed by Deborah Brash/Brash Design
Set in 11/13.5 pt Goudy Old Style by Midland Typesetters.
Maryborough, Victoria
Printed and bound in Australia by
Southwood Press, Marrickville, NSW

5 4

ARTISTS MAKE DREAMS
FOR THOSE
WHO ARE AWAKE.

Plato

Dream Dictionary Introduction

We all have dreams or at least one dream that we can't forget; a dream that haunts us or keeps niggling at us, often for years after the dream occurs. The dream continues to appear in vivid detail—every colour, scent and event; it floods us with the same intense feelings that we awoke with at the time we first had the dream.

We are expected to be consoled by parental explanations of it being 'just a dream', only to find that dismissing it as 'nothing', doesn't in fact lessen the nagging feeling that drives us to want to get to the bottom of it's true meaning. This wasn't always the case. Ancient Western and native cultures recognised dreams as the 'television network' that the spirit or non-physical 'side' uses to give us guidance on matters about our health, general well-being, personal happiness and future. Only in the Dark and Middle Ages did Western civilisations come to believe that we were too insignificant to receive direct communications from a deity or higher being and all dreams were therefore dismissed as heretical delusions. Nevertheless, our dreams continued to niggle and nag us until once again we were encouraged to take them seriously when Freud suggested that dreams were the manifestations of our unconscious conflicts or frustrated and repressed desires.

You might call the source or inspiration of dreams, your subconscious; or your right-brain; someone else may call it God; or, as we do in this book, it can be called your Dream Teacher, your Dream Guide, your Future Self or Higher Self. The name you give to this inspiration is far less important than the realisation that our dreams can reveal to us every aspect of ourselves or our lives: anything in need of healing, re-thinking, especially the areas where we need to take appropriate action. This is the one aspect of dreams that all dream theorists agree on, despite having differing opinions about the source of our dreams.

Given the importance of the information that dreams reveal to us about ourselves, no wonder most people immediately ask why our Dream Teacher doesn't come straight out and say 'This is your current issue and here is the solution.' The answer is that the intricate and peculiar right-brain language of dreams communicates directly with our emotions.

To the Eastern mind, which is open to more intricate right-brain influences, this question would not arise; Eastern culture and religious practices are rich sources of right-brain stimulation. The same is true in other ways for all the indigenous peoples of the world. For Anglo-Saxons and European or Mediterranean cultures, however, the left-brain tends to overrule and ration-alise, often dismissing the validity of our feelings, emotions and instinctive information from the more intuitive right-brain. This has led Western society to some pretty convoluted, weird, and wonderfully off-skew interpretations of the meanings of dreams.

The fact is that we probably wouldn't perceive, feel, listen to, or take on board this information from our Dream Teacher if they gave it to us 'straight'. We humans don't as a general rule like the crystal-clear, plain truth about our innermost fears and insecurities told to us straight. Just think back to a time that you tried to tell a friend a home truth, with all the best intentions, and you'll identify with the dilemma our Higher Self is confronted with nightly. We tend to most appreciate our inner revelations and truths when we come to them ourselves, step by step, little by little. That's why our dreams can, at first glance, seem like befuddled, bizarre mazes designed by incoherent lunatics.

Our Higher Self knows better than we do that our attention is more effectively held and motivated, or geared to contemplate the intrinsic significance, when inspired by a gripping visual. That is why it's often the emotional charge or the content of our dreams that first needs to be acknowledged if we wish to understand and resolve the issue that the dream is directly addressing.

Often we dream of the new and exciting ways we could be focusing our inner and outer search for personal fulfilment. In our dreams, everything that is held in the subconscious mind or suppressed in the unconscious mind is open to us. In dreams we constantly review our past, especially as we look at old emotional responses in our relationships. Other dreams help us to focus on our present needs, clear current emotional issues and prepare ourselves for the future, both material and spiritual, while our vast intelligence filters and mulls over the significance of the symbols in each and every dream—even those we don't consciously recall.

Understanding the symbols of your dreams makes that much easier the journey towards greater understanding of yourself and life in general. Your Dream Guide will still present you with bizarre visions that would be the envy of Frederico Fellini or Orson Welles but at least you will begin to understand the language and crack the code to your unconscious motivations and unhealthy fears.

Interpreting Your Own Dreams

The symbols and signs listed in this handbook are not all universal. Because we each have our own unique feelings or attitudes to a various range of images, your personal symbols often become your dream symbols and it's the special connection you have with a particular symbol that should always be incorporated into your general reading of dream symbols. Variances occur because of the way we individually relate to our environment, suburb, family history and all the other factors that make us uniquely ourselves.

For instance, chocolate for most people would symbolise something sweet, indulgent, or rewarding. However, if you had a chocolate frenzy as a child that rendered you sick for days, it would mean something totally different—probably indulgence beyond what's healthy. If then you had a dream that featured chocolate as one of its symbols, it would, when put in context with the other symbols in your dreamscape, be a warning against indulging in 'something' that might be self-pity, drugs or any other issue in your life at the time.

This is why the very best person to analyse your dreams is always you. Only you intimately know your feelings and attitudes to every symbol; only you know exactly what is taking place in your life at that given moment, or what has taken place in your past. Your Dream Guide will use, wherever possible, specific personal symbols that will conjure up strong emotional responses from your own memory banks and personal experience. Of course, there is so much more that your Dream Guide wants to point out to you that may fall outside your personal experience and feelings. Sometimes your Dream Teacher will resort to universal symbols in the hope that you will soon find a way to access their meaning in your waking life.

The first rule of dream interpretation is to incorporate your own instinctive attitudes and feelings about the symbols with the ones listed in the book. Your personal dream interpretation, when put into correct context with the events of your waking life, will instantly tell you if your 'picture' is accurate.

Another key to analysing your dreams accurately is recognising that almost every dream character (besides those known to you *intimately*) is almost always a manifestation or a component of yourself, your fears, your behaviour or your attitudes that has been symbolically 'put in the spotlight'. The characteristics of the person in your dream therefore symbolise the characteristics of either this component of yourself or your behaviour. For instance, the dark-coated, shadowy stalker always lurking in your dreams, would represent a part of you that you don't want to see, yet is always there behind you. Likewise, the little boy or girl crying in the cellar is the emotional inner child that you have kept hidden and perhaps stopped nurturing. Even animals for the most part represent aspects of yourself, although it's always worth checking an animal dream in the dictionary. By 'free-associating' or writing down the first words that pop into your head in relation to any dream symbol, you will gain a greater understanding of what this particular dream means for you.

The Steps

Analyse your dreams by putting *all* the dream symbols down on paper and write next to each one what this symbol means to you personally. Remember, your dreams are like a jigsaw puzzle: each piece is nothing on its own—only when you put all the pieces together properly can you see the big picture.

Next, write down the emotional essence of your dream: how did you feel in the dream—sad, scared, happy, joyous, angry, stressed, secretive, resentful, bewildered, or out of control? If you went through a series of emotions, list each of your emotions as they came up, next to the dream symbol.

Make sure you don't overlook important dream symbols such as the dream setting, the action, your dream characters, the time of day, what the weather was like and anything else such as smells you noticed; or what sounds you heard, if any.

And most important of all, be honest with yourself about your true feelings: how you feel about your life, your relationships, your future career, and especially how you felt about yourself at the time of the dream.

For example, avid dreamer Frank Saint, from Tasmania sent in this interesting dream:

> I was moving house from a strange illogical space above the altar inside a church, to a spacious room nearby, which resembled a classroom. It was on the first floor, where it overlooked a big beautiful lake with an old city in the background. I felt extremely joyous, relaxed and happy; there was also a reassuring sense of familiarity.
>
> I cannot ever remember feeling so good after a dream.

Frank was so emotionally moved and elated by this dream that he willingly added his personal associations to the symbols in his dream.

Symbol	Emotion	Personal Meaning
Moving house	Relaxed	Moving = change/move out of my old shell.
		House = where I live.
Above the altar	Strange	Above = overview/the space within the church where God alone presides.
		Altar = sacrifice
Spacious room	Happy	Spacious room = new space/a fresh start/a new world/a clean slate.
Classroom	Open, spacious, bare	Classroom = inner space of knowing ignorance/unlearning.
First floor	Height, space, open and light	First floor = accessible to girls only, in my primary school.
Overlooking	Home, unity, empowering	Overlooking = observation/the big picture.
Beautiful lake	Calm, harmony, it felt intimate	Beautiful lake = very clean water.
Old city	Familiar	Old city = a stone tower/old 'feel' to it.

Frank's dream interpretation in his own symbolic language is thus: Frank is moving from the place where his real inner self ('the place where I live',) resides, (above the altar) which for some reason he's been removed from; or perhaps he's (above) everyone, because of some of his (strange) religious or self (sacrificial) beliefs.

The place where he is moving to within himself will give him more room or a (spaciousness or space) to start ('moving out of my old shell') and/or express himself, in a place where he will be (making a fresh start) on a (new slate).

He is (happy) in this (new world). Frank will learn much in this dream (classroom) and his feminine right-brain will become more (accessible), as symbolised by (girls only on the first floor). This brings with it a (calming) influence especially to his current emotional state as symbolised by (the lake); he realises the right-brain gift of true (intimacy), hence the (clear water).

Here in this dream, he can clearly see the (bigger picture) of his life and his purpose. He reconnects to the (space) (where God alone presides), and he will be totally safe doing so. Frank now gains an (overview) of his life, finding a (unity) and spiritually 'coming (home)' to the (familiar old city) as a symbol of his ancient instinctive wisdom.

Once you crack the code of your personal dream symbols you will open up an inner resource that in time can allow you to overcome your fears, liberate you from stress dis-ease (unease), realise your own power, expand your personal skills and put you in direct contact with the vast, all-knowing you.

How to Recall Dreams

Many people claim not to dream at all or not to be able to recall any of their dreams, yet it's been proven that we all dream during a seven to eight hour sleep cycle which at the very least is one to one and half hours a night. Not being able to recall your dreams is usually the result of either being brutally awoken by an alarm clock, dashing into the shower and into your daily routine; or by being dragged out of sleep by small children. By the time you recall you have been dreaming, the details have once again slipped back to the unconscious part of yourself. Sometimes it happens because the individual intentionally doesn't want to remember or know what is going on in the deep unseen crevices within them.

The first step in recalling your dreams is to decide consciously that you want to remember them. An excellent way to do this, is to buy yourself a blank book or dream diary that you keep beside your bed with a pen. As a conscious physical act, you are affirming to your subconscious that you now wish to recall your dreams. On waking, even if it's in the middle of the night, write a brief, point-form description of the events of the dream and your feelings. Don't jump out of bed immediately; it helps to lie still in the position you slept; and allow the dream images to come back to you.

If you still struggle, start by practising on the weekend when you will not be woken by an alarm and try to eat a *light* meal rather than a heavy meal before 8 pm and three hours before you go to sleep. Also refrain from taking alcohol and drugs, including prescription drugs.

As you get more proficient with your dream recall, it's also useful to meditate consciously before you sleep or to ask your Dream Teacher to help you recall your dreams. With practice and patience, we can all easily remember and understand our dreams which in turn will inspire us to fulfil ourselves in ways that continually help us to be more relaxed, happier and freer in our waking lives.

Half a Pound of Dream Dictionary and an Ounce of Commonsense

When you interpret your dreams using a dream dictionary, a word of warning: a dream dictionary can never encompass the millions of symbols that are available to you or the very personal associations you have with them. It can only ever be used as a guide to interpreting your personal dream symbols. Supplement this with your own experience, so make sure you consider what the symbols mean in *your* life, particularly when the meaning given in the dream dictionary doesn't seem appropriate to you or your dream.

Once you've been interpreting your dreams and dream symbols for a while, you'll find that many of the meanings become second nature, and your commonsense and intuition will often provide the right connection before you need to reach for the dictionary. Allow the dictionary to inspire you; remember to associate your symbol with the universal symbols till you discover something you relate to, yet hadn't realised before.

Examine the clues in your various dream scenarios, especially those that the characters, setting and action provide. Within each dream you will find your personal symbols, and an emotional response; check these with the dictionary to expand your dream messages till they make perfect sense and feel accurate. Probably the most complex to interpret are the universal symbols, as so many of the associations we have with these symbols are buried in the past. Part of the reason that dreams seem so 'weird' is that many of the people and objects have symbolic rather than literal meanings. Dream dictionaries are valuable in providing a guide to these numerous universal associations. With a little interest and further research you can discover many more of these associations and connections and with practise you will find that most, if not all, of your dreams will unfold valuable insights.

Interpreting your own dreams is like learning a whole new language—the language of symbols. For example, the churning ocean in your dreams could really be a sign of your churning emotions, whereas the frolicking horse may represent your sexual playfulness. With such a myriad of dream symbols to choose from, dream interpreting can seem rather daunting at first. Since they can help us in so many ways, it is natural to want to remember even more of our dreams. In fact, the dreams we recall spontaneously and easily, are those with a particular significance; they usually come in a form which will grab our attention (such as a nightmare) or a bizarre riddle you can't work out. It is a good idea to record these dreams and to heed the messages provided, as they are valuable clues to resolving the current issues in your life.

While there are many things you can do to improve dream recall, three ingredients guarantee success: interest, intention and time. Many people who become teachers do so because they love to impart knowledge to someone else, especially someone who wants to learn. Your Higher Self is such a teacher; and you will discover that as you show an interest in remembering and analysing your dreams, you are opening the lid to a treasure trove of information, perhaps more than you could possibly find the time to analyse in a single day.

Intention is just a consolidation of interest, and intent represents the commitment we make to studying the content of our dreams. Most people do this normally and naturally. You can aid this natural function by deciding to record your dreams for a while. By doing this, you are really just establishing your intention. Sometimes this is all that is needed to open you up to a deluge of dreams.

Establishing a dream diary reinforces your intention. Whether you buy the cheapest notepad form a stationery store, or invest in a beautiful leather-bound diary, keep it beside your bed so you can record your dreams in it as soon as you wake. I began my first dream diary whilst staying with my mother in Queensland: the dog would wake me each morning at first light, wanting to be let out for his morning walk. In the 10 minutes or so that the dog was out, I began to jot down my dreams. Then I would go back to sleep for another hour and jot down another dream. After a few weeks I could see definite patterns emerging, and then I would have a dream that did not fit the pattern, or one that disturbed me emotionally. Some were so weird I had no idea what to make of them. Years later their importance is clear and I'm always pleased I took the trouble to write them down; not only did I acquire a good habit, but also the same or similar symbols continue to act as signposts in my life today.

The third ingredient is time: make sure you allow yourself enough time to write down your dreams and interpret them. When you remember your dreams more easily and regularly, you may decide just to mentally check them for messages, without writing them down—writing the message instead. Initially you will find that the practice of keeping a dream diary assists you in remembering your dreams, and provides a useful record you can refer back to, when checking the 'feel' and accuracy of any prophetic dreams you may have.

Vicki makes the following comment about remembering her dreams:

I find nowadays that my dreams are there, close to the surface, every time I wake up. Providing I don't rush out of bed to answer the phone, or turn my attention too quickly onto planning my day, it's just a matter of reaching out and grabbing the dream memory. Then I have a choice—I can either lie in bed and interpret it, and maybe reinforce it by telling it to my partner, or else if it seems particularly significant I write it down.

The significant ones for me are those that give me a new way of looking at things or are particularly creative or beautiful, and also those that pack an emotional punch. The emotions in this sort often stay with me for the rest of the day, like an altered state of consciousness. This is great if it's a dream about hot sex, but not so much fun if it's a nightmare. As for my dream diary, it's just a little soft-cover notebook that I keep beside my bed. I never thought to decorate it with pictures and doodles like Quentin's—but it does me, and it's great to refer back to.

Write down whatever fragments of a dream are in your mind when you wake. Once you begin your dream diary you'll discover personal symbols and interpretations become specific messages in your waking life.

Learning to trust your own intuition is a far more valuable tool than any dream handbook can ever be. I think that one of the most interesting things about using a dream dictionary is that your Higher Self will send you symbols you actually know and are familiar with, in some form. In fact, any belief you currently hold will be re-played in your dreams. The dictionary that works for you will continue to do that for as long as the symbols make sense and assist you in your waking life.

Whether your dreams have lots of symbols or a few, ask yourself, 'What does this symbol mean to me?' If it is an object, explore it's visual characteristics as well as its functions. Take a garden hose, for example. A Freudian dream dictionary might liken it to a penis, because of its phallic shape and the way water spurts out of it; a Jungian dictionary will include the symbolism of the hose as the universal snake, an archetype (an inherited idea or mode of thought, derived from the experience of the race and present in the unconscious of the individual, controlling their way of perceiving the world).

For accurate dream analysis you also need to take in cultural aspects and the function of the dream symbol in your current waking life. To most Australian children, a hose could also represent cleansing and cooling, particularly if you happen to associate it with having fun on hot days when you were young. Other associations you might make are: the water used use to 'hose' ourselves; the action, as to wash off the dirt; to water the garden; in general, hoses are used to wash cars, boats, trailers, caravans, etc. It could even relate to the nurturing aspect of the water itself, if you are hosing a dream garden. Which plants or flowers, vegetables or fruits that you water may be the important dream symbol that holds the message in your dream. It's also possible that the person holding the hose is the vital clue in your dream; especially if it happens to be the 'hoser poser' stickybeak neighbour who knows everything about everyone in your street.

The Emotional Connection

If you can't work out which explanation works for your dream, then the most important clue will be your emotional response to the dream. When you experience any powerful emotional response in your dream, it is likely to be an 'emotional release' dream. Emotional release dreams can be ones where you find yourself joyously hacking your boss to pieces to feed a pack of waiting sharks; crying about the loss of someone you have no memory of ever knowing in waking life, or cringing in fear and loathing before the masked figure wielding an axe, who advances towards you step by step. From these dreams you may wake up in a cold sweat, screaming in fear, or trembling with vented rage. Such dreams are actually an inventive yet highly effective form of stress release. When you understand the meaning of your dream, you will generally have an emotional response as well as a mental 'Ah ha!' and you will then know you are on track in your interpretation—it 'feels' right. Be both practical as well as mystical, use your left- and right-brain power to discover the true meaning of your dreams for yourself.

Everything we have ever experienced is within us. This information is accessible either when we are in a deep sleep, or during any trance-like meditation, or when we are completely relaxed or under hypnosis. At these times, we can easily recall all of our past experiences (including our past lifetimes). At this time, the mind's entire contents, the conscious, unconscious, subconscious, and superconscious, become completely available to us. It is also one of the few times our physical body actually gets to speak its mind.

Our dreams will show us not only our present focus, and whether that is currently a physical/material, emotional, mental or spiritual one, but also any incomplete issues from the past that need to be resolved before we can move on to the next step in our current waking life. Once we are in the right place at the right time, our dreams will become more prophetic and assist us to take advantage of our future opportunities.

Most of our dreams are asking us to look at ourselves from a different perspective. For instance, if you never express anger, you may dream of being enraged by someone or something. When you hide your sadness, you may wake up in tears. Dreams are frequently showing you things about yourself that you don't or won't confront in your waking life. Some dreams can solve our current problems and help inspire us to take appropriate action. Others alert us to anything that is unhealthy in our personal relationships. When we make the right connections, and solve the riddles of our dreams, we make the right decisions in our lives— decisions relating to the values we choose to embrace, how we communicate and express ourselves in our relationships, our present life choices and how they influence where we want to go next.

Our dream settings are always fascinating. Every mountain and precipice, each abode and every path, is a rich tapestry of symbols woven together to create a complete message for us personally. It's valuable to consider the many nuances of your dream settings, particularly those things you were drawn to. When you've identified your dream setting, ask yourself, 'Do I know this place?' 'What does it remind me of?' 'When was I there?' 'Who was with me at that time?'

Your dream may occur in a location you're already familiar with, particularly somewhere you've lived—especially during the significant first seven years of life, when our personality develops. This is frequently a 'time warp' dream, one that alerts you to a particular time scale in your life. The purpose of time-warp dreams is to inspire you to work on resolving an issue that stems from this time in your life.

Dreamers and Sceptics

Why do some people firmly believe they never dream, whilst others are avid dreamers, able to recall almost all of their dreams? The answer lies in brain usage. We each use an individual balance of the left- and right-brain functions and abilities. In the late 1950s scientists began to unravel the mystery of our two distinct brain hemispheres, and their different functions. These two hemispheres work in partnership, enhancing and complementing each other. The connecting brain stems of each hemisphere cross over at the base of the brain to govern the central nervous system of the opposite side of the body. Thus the left side of your brain coordinates the right side of your body. This side of the brain is responsible for your logical and rational thought processes, which we frequently refer to as the masculine side because these attributes have often been assigned to the male in our society. The right brain, connected to the left side of the body, is the site of intuition and inspiration. It governs the receptivity of emotional information, hence its relationship to the feminine.

Avid dreamers obviously access more right-brain functions, and the so-called non-dreamers are more firmly entrenched in left-brain activities. But, why can't we all learn to use the whole of our brain and have an equal balance and ability to use more brain power?

If we look at a general cross-section of Western society, we find that left-brain functions have become increasingly dominant since the industrial revolution, while the right-brain is often unacknowledged or unexpressed in our lives. It's interesting that our dreams are one of the few right-brain activities we can't totally suppress. By understanding our dreams, we learn to trust the intuitive impulses that spring from the right-brain, to consciously incorporate them into our lives.

The setting of your dreamscape is also significant, because the right-brain allows you to appreciate beauty, balance, colour, movement and form. Some dreams are straightforward and easy to interpret: they are often action-packed, and seem to be quite logical or rational; they are influenced by the left-brain. Bizarre dream scenarios arise when your intuitive right-brain wants more expression. When this happens, dreams can become quite confusing and disturbing.

The eastern Yin/Yang symbol is a good visual example of the balance between the left- and right-brain. It represents the duality of opposite forces: masculine/feminine, creative/receptive and active/passive in constant motion, creating an interplay of opposites whilst constantly retaining its balance—like the two sides of the brain ceaselessly involved and interacting with each other, yet separate entities with a very different focus. This duality of life is the essence of change, and change is the only constant thing in the universe.

Dream Lessons

For most people, the type of dream most commonly remembered is the dream lesson. It is in this area that remembering our dreams can be of immense value: the messages from our Higher Selves that are otherwise available only to our subconscious minds are brought closer to our conscious awareness. Dream lessons ask us to be aware or—beware—of our motivations and encourage us in our new ventures, whilst continually revealing the issues we are currently tackling in our lives.

This dream lesson was recorded by Sue, in Western Australia.

I was on a journey with a group of Christians. I was considered weird because I was into all sorts of esoteric things. [This is true—I actually feel rather out of place with most Christians, like I'm on a different wavelength, even though I was brought up a Protestant.] We were trekking through a desert area with few trees. One girl there particularly had it in for me. I warned her about bee stings, but she didn't believe me. Then she was stung on the right side of the face by a large, fat bee. Someone pulled the bee off her and showed it to her. Her face had begun going red with inflammation and she was in a lot of pain. I took her aside and performed a psychic healing on her, which reduced the pain a lot, but still left a red mark on her cheek. After this we became friends.

The dream location is a desert, so can represent something we've 'deserted', or left behind us. It is also often a sign of an area in our own lives that we've neglected. There is little growth—this emphasis on a lack of growth is supported by the mention of an absence of trees, as trees represent growth and development (and even influential people) in the dream scenario. Everything from our dreams has a meaning, even minor details like this. This is why it helps to be thorough in recording your dreams. Later when you interpret them, take the time to explore carefully all the symbols you have made reference to. Here we find Sue on a journey through the desert with a group of Christians; we see her feeling of isolation within this group. Sue has felt 'deserted' by the Christian fellowship of her childhood—yet a link with it still remains.

In examining the characters, we find a girl and a bee. The girl 'has it in' for Sue—suggesting that Sue is feeling 'attacked' by someone in her life at the moment, possibly someone she identifies as being a Christian. This girl is attracting a lot of anger towards herself; inflammation is usually a sign of anger, so the girl is 'smarting', probably as a result of people's responses to her animosity. The bee is an animal which stings only in self-defence, showing Sue how this particular girl attracts defensive reactions from other people, and then feels hurt by these reactions. Through the dream, the Christian girl becomes linked to Sue's esoteric healing ability in a union of friendship and nurturing, rather than the initial hostility of ignorance and separation. This is a message to Sue to use her natural healing talents to mend the relationship between them. By making the first move and reaching out to this other girl, she'll be able to turn the current strained relationship into a supportive friendship.

Fears and Fantasies

Quite often our dreams will serve us by bringing up into our conscious mind the fears and fantasies we have hidden from ourselves, especially childhood ones that lie deeply buried in our subconscious minds.

For instance, someone with arachnophobia may dream about reaching into a bag full of spiders, or a happily married person may find themselves with a passionate dream lover. You may dream that you arrive late for a job interview and don't know how to answer any of the questions. Or that you are stark naked in a shopping plaza; even going to the toilet in the middle of a football field. These are all quite common themes in fear dreams. In fact, as you face these fears night after night in your dream time, you will access your inner courage and move through the fears you face in your waking life with more ease.

Prophetic Dreams

At some time, we will all experience a prophetic dream about ourselves and/or those close to us. These prophetic dreams often help us to avoid ugly situations. The purpose of a prophecy is to avert any potential disaster or to warn us to change something in our lives. The purpose of other types of prophetic dreams is to help you to correct one of your unconscious negative patterns, such as a tendency to be late for important meetings, or a fear of making a commitment. Remember, these dreams are showing you probable realities: don't fear them, they are encouraging you to change and their purpose is to shake you from a fatalistic view of life.

In some prophetic dreams, your Higher Self will warn you of something so that you can assist someone else. For instance, you may dream that your child is run over, only to be horrified to discover this has actually happened to someone you know. The reason you receive a dream like this is to give you instant empathy with the person at the time of their loss and through their subsequent grieving. If and when you do have dreams like this one, you have discovered how to 'walk a mile in another man's moccasins' as native Americans say.

It's a good idea to cultivate this gift and it may appear at any stage in life, as Mary Jane, a Canadian living in Indonesia, discovered about her strong prophetic senses. Over the past year, her interest in channelling psychic information and dreams has blossomed to become a major focus of her days.

During this time, she received the following dream:

> *I am going to a doctor's appointment with a child who has a tumour. I see a sign saying 'RS', and next to it a left arrow. [In Mary Jane's personal system of dream interpretation, left indicates the 'wrong' path, or a mistake.] I remember thinking: RS, Rumah Sakit, the Indonesian word for hospital. I was worried about the outcome of the appointment, and said a small prayer.*

Less than a week later, Mary Jane's daughter phoned from Canada to announce that her husband (whose initials are RS) had just come out of major surgery. This surgery had been necessary to correct a mistake made by a physician during an earlier operation, that involved removing a tumour.

Two nights after receiving this dream, Mary Jane then dreamed:

> *My son and wife had their baby [Mary Jane's daughter-in-law was pregnant at the time of this dream], but the baby looked like one of my nephews. As I did up his diaper, I commented that he sure looked like his father. All the cousins and relatives were present, but my niece was wearing black, and her mother [Mary Jane's sister-in-law, who lead her into many of her psychic pursuits] was in a green dress.*

A few days later, Mary Jane was told that the one-month old son of her niece (the woman wearing black in her dream) had died, and the funeral had taken place on the day preceding Mary Jane's dream. All of the cousins from her dream were present at the funeral.

Dreams like these lend strong support to the belief that psychic and prophetic information frequently enter our dreams, particularly where loss or sadness touches people who are close to our hearts. In Mary Jane's case, she was connecting with both the current and near-future events affecting her family. These were not things she was able to change, but because of these dreams, a part of her conscious mind was aware of her family's situation. This allowed her to process in dream time some of her own emotions and reactions to these events, and she could then more effectively deal with them and support her family in her waking life.

Déjà Vu

Déjà vu is an experience that all of us have occasionally. It's the feeling that we are walking in our own footsteps, as if we have just stepped into a play that we already know by heart, or that somehow we've 'lived this scene before'—literally, 'been there, done that'. It explains that sense of replay that occurs when we find ourselves in a situation we know we haven't been in during our waking life, yet where we instantly recognise some of the surroundings, the participants or the action taking place. People who experience a lot of *déjà vu* often don't recall their dreams until they relive them: that is, when they get the feeling, 'I've done this before', they probably have—in their dreams.

The prophetic nature of dreams has been recognised and respected by many cultures, and dreams have often played a significant role in the decision-making process within these cultures. A great example of this comes from native American tradition, where the initiation ceremony of a Vision Quest is undertaken by initiates to attune with the Great Spirit and receive spiritual, emotional, mental and physical gifts of power and protection from the spirit-world and Mother Earth.

Love and Stuff

Relationship dreams are by far the most prolific and pertinent to our personal development. They alert us to new points of view, or force us to realise our true feelings about these people and situations.

Dreams involving your intimate nearest and dearest are such amazing inner creations! Not only can they guide our lives and loves, but they also warn us of impending disasters, bringing conscious awareness to our greatest fears or fantasies. They also deliver practical advice, sage-like wisdom and universal truth, inspiring us to take responsibility for everything that we have the power to change in our waking lives.

This dream from Fiona Allen, of the Australian Capital Territory, shows us how clothing clearly revealed the truth of the situation in one of her past relationships.

> *My ex-boyfriend was wearing a dress (floral with a yellow back ground). I tried to take it off him—I don't think it was a sexual thing (i.e. to get his clothes off). The way I see it is that the dress, being yellow, represents friendship and shows that if he were female, I could be friends with him (we started out as friends).*

What wisdom! In this dream Fiona's ex-boyfriend is symbolised as someone who is not what she really wants. She tries to change him, (take the dress off him). Her interpretation is correct, as yellow is often associated with the mind and mental faculties. They are no longer in a romantic physical or emotional relationship, yet there is a chance they could continue to share their genuine love and respect for each other either mentally or spiritually.

Home Sweet Home

When you dream about a house or home it will universally represent your self—your authentic self. Each room relates to an aspect of your self, and the functions you associate with each room will give you more clues to work with. When you find extra rooms in your dream house, it represents the aspects of your future self and your hidden talents, as well as your hidden personality traits and any current waking life situations.

Food and Festivities

Perhaps more than anything else, food holds very personal associations. Just imagine the different connections a juicy steak has for a vegetarian, compared with a committed carnivore. Use your intuition to see what message your latest culinary dream delight holds for you.

You may be aware that any food which is high in carbohydrates is likely to stimulate dreaming. Hence the term 'spaghetti dreams'.

It's often only during sleep that your body speaks its mind. Anything that aggravates your stomach often wafts its way up into your dreams in the form of a warning. Maybe you'll dream that the lamington you devoured for afternoon tea is engulfing you in its soft jammy centre. Have you considered that perhaps from your stomach's point of view it is? And your body is now letting you know the effects of your excesses—in no uncertain terms. This is especially true in children's dreams, so assist them to listen to their body and be grateful for the learning experience a food-related nightmare can bring.

The Morning After

Dreams about sickness have one important aim: to warn us, and keep us healthy. They can sometimes be early warnings of illness, often providing that crucial piece of information or the practical or mystical remedy that could bring about healing.

Physical illness and injury dreams have the potential to become prophetic—if we ignore them. By alerting us, these dreams of body dis-ease (unease) can be taken as early warning symptoms. If we can effectively avert the disaster in our waking lives, we are in fact practising one of the most effective preventative medicines.

Here's an example of a body-speak dream, from Jeff of Western Australia.

I was going to participate in a yoga class. But when I looked down at my legs, I saw that the fronts of my legs above the knees were covered in huge warty lumps. There was a particularly big growth on my left leg, just above the knee. I was worried about what people would think if they saw them, so I was wondering what clothes I could wear to cover the lumps. At the same time, I was hoping I'd be able to heal myself.

Poor Jeff. Warty growths (a sign of anger, self-hatred, guilt or deep resentment) have sprung up all over his thighs. Since our legs carry us through life it would be reasonable to surmise that Jeff's anger, self-hatred or guilt, as depicted by the warts, are impeding his ability to go forward in life in the direction that he truly wants.

The large growth near his left knee is also very interesting. Problems in the knee area metaphysically represent a stubborn ego and pride, while the left side of the body represents receptivity or the female, right-brain energy. When we combine these two symbols we can see that Jeff may be unnecessarily suffering because his ego and pride prevent him from listening to and receiving the help or advice that can help him banish the anger that is stopping him from moving forward in his life. Alternatively, the large growth or warts (his self-hatred) may relate to a specific issue or pattern in his relationships with women.

Jeff feels uncomfortable and worries that other people will notice; he searches for what clothing (attitudes) he can use to mask his resentment. At the same time he wants to heal himself of this anger which no doubt in time he will—particularly as his Higher Self has now given him the clues through which he can identify and source the cause of what he most needs to heal within.

In our society we're often taught to put other people's needs before our own, that it's 'bad' to be selfish. We work against a lot of conditioning just asking for our basic needs to be met. This is an important dream for Jeff: as he learns to acknowledge his true feelings, release his pride and stubbornness and the issues he has with women, he will begin his inner process of self-healing. The yoga would definitely give his energy and aliveness a boost, to say nothing of the 'babes' he's bound to meet at a yoga class!

Scattered through this dictionary are some of the more common points of injury, and their metaphysical—emotional basis, for you to use as a guideline in your dream interpretations. Many of them are expressed by Louise L Hay in her book *You Can Heal Your Life*, in which she also gives the positive affirmations to assist with the healing of each physical ailment.

Her earlier book, *Heal Your Body*, is recommended for not only understanding your dream ailments, but your physical ones as well.

Dreams are far more than night-time fantasies, sent to amuse and confuse us. They carry a lot of valuable information which we can easily learn to access and use in our daily lives. If we don't remember or bother to interpret our dreams, it doesn't mean they are not working. But for those of us who do, there can be an enormous amount of 'food for thought' contained in our dreams.

The benefits of problem-solving or creative dreams are obvious today, and it is natural for all of us to have such inspired dreams from time to time. You may have noticed that often you feel better about a problem after a night's sleep, even if you don't recall dreaming. This is where the phrase 'to sleep on it' comes from. Are there ways in which we can harness this power of our dreams to provide solutions to our daily problems and emotional dramas? Luckily for us, the answer is 'yes'. These solutions are not just a matter of chance, they are healing or teaching dreams that can actually be 'incubated' along certain topic lines and themes.

Pregnancy and Birth

Dreams about giving birth, attending a birth, being stuck in tunnels—in fact, any dreams where you find yourself feeling physically trapped, or as if someone or something is sitting on your chest—are symbolic representations of birth memories. These dream themes generally occur at times when we are experiencing any major change in our waking lives. Both men and women dream of birth and giving birth. Since we all experienced it, we all have an unconscious cellular-level body memory of our own birth. Sometimes dreamers can re-create exactly their personal 'birth script' in a dream. Dreams of birth can herald an actual pregnancy and the subsequent birth of your child. Usually they relate to your new ideas or the birth of a new project. They may represent a higher or more experienced part of yourself coming to life. During times when major changes are taking place in life you might dream your physical 'birth-script'. Pregnant women do dream prolifically, but then they are indeed dreaming for two.

Modes of Transport

Have you ever found yourself in your dream time, travelling aboard some weird or wonderful means of transport? Maybe it was just the family car, or a rickety bicycle, a sky-diving plane, the express train, the local school bus, the Daimler Dart you have always lusted after, or even a sinking ship. Each type of transport we encounter in our dream holds the same message: all are expressions of the way we move ourselves through life. Are you still chugging, full steam ahead, along the narrow tracks of your childhood conditioning, or are you the symbolic donkey laden down with burdens, struggling up the steep mountain pass? Perhaps you are the one exploring new horizons in your latest creative endeavour, the self-propelled flying machine? Your dream cars or other vehicles reveal to you how you currently 'transport' yourself through your life. Whichever medium you choose, some general rules apply.

A bright pink Cadillac could be a very romantic image, but if the seats turn out to be made of hessian bags, this image may be only skin-deep. Watch out also for the car's phallic nature—particularly when you find yourself being chased by your boyfriend's long, red, shiny Porsche!

Vicki recorded the following 'transporting' dream in her journal, at a time when she was facing an important career decision:

> *I am on a trail. There are many paths and many modes of transport. Intuitively I take the middle road, and later the map confirms it to be the correct path. Then I must swim across a salt-water [brackish] river, which lies right next to a freshwater river. It is brown and fast-running. In the next scene I am on a train. Other people from the trail have stopped early and set up camp. I see topless women and men, camping happily beside the railway. I decide to keep going, and see a semi-trailer has crashed, plummeting over a cliff that rises up to my right.*

Vicki has made a list of the dream symbols and their personal meaning plus her emotional response.

Symbol	Emotion	Personal Meaning
Trail	Curious	Life's purpose
Many paths	Confusion	Which way to go
Modes of transport	Choices	Which one to use
Intuitive	Gut feelings	Proves to be right
Middle path	Balanced	Between two aspects
Fresh water river	Nurturing	Irrigating, feeding
Salt-water river	Brackish	Saline, dark
Must swim	Compelled	Have to swim
Train	Movement	Train of thought
Others set up camp	Interest	Settlement
Topless women	Nurturing	Homely
Keep going	Motivation	Move on
Semi-trailer over cliff	Fear of unknown	Out of control

The (trail) in Vicki's dream is a sign of her ongoing journey through life. Here she uses many different means (forms of transport) to learn her life lessons and reach her full potential. Faced with her current career decision, she (intuitively) takes the correct (path), this being the (middle road)—a colloquialism for any conservative path. Taking the middle road also suggests a balance between the emotional left path (the feminine right-brain) and the logical right path (the masculine left-brain). This middle path leads her (across) a (fast-running) and (brown, brackish river), an indication that at this time in her life she must (swim), or wade through her darker emotions (brackish indicating unclear, hidden or base emotions), rather than be swept away by them. One of Vicki's options at the time was a project to which she had a great emotional attachment, although her final choice took her against the stream of these emotions, onto a more balanced path.

Vicki's dream journey continues on a (train), a sign that she's on the same (path) or track that many other people travel. Here she continues and (goes beyond) where (most people stop), realising that she is not yet ready to (camp down) and have a family—the (topless women) to her signify motherhood. (Semi-trailers) are cumbersome vehicles and a sign to Vicki to beware of overloading herself in her new project, lest she also (crash) in her (unknown) new objectives.

Planes

Up, up and away! Planes are a sign that you are either moving very fast in your life (symbolised by their immense speed; covering vast distances and fast travel) or that you are beginning to astral-travel—this is especially true when your dream plane doesn't take off from an airport and you just find yourself in a plane. Plane dreams also suggest that you're moving from a local to a global focus, definitely freeing yourself with a good understanding and accurate awareness of what you're doing—due to the height at which you fly. Sometimes you need to beware! A plane in a nose-dive is a sure sign that life is moving out of control fast, and in the wrong direction, As Nick, of Queensland, was to discover with his dream:

> I am in a plane that is having difficulties, I ask if I have time to go to the toilet first, but the air steward says, 'No, go to your cot', and he points to a series of chairs facing to the side of the plane instead of to the front. They face in towards a high table, rather like at a conference or even high chairs. I ask if I need a seat-belt, but he says no. Then the plane dives down at a terrifying speed and I see us fly amidst Brisbane's high-rise buildings (I was born in Brisbane). I decide there is no way we will survive, but then the plane pulls out of its nose-dive, circles around, and begins a second horrific dive. Then I wake up.

This is almost like a *déjà vu* experience for Nick. The second nose-dive suggests that this is not the first time in his life that he's felt out of control—it's definitely a time to reclaim his own power in guiding his future. There are quite a few references to Nick's early childhood here—the cot, toilet-training, a high chair with a belt to hold the baby in, and his home city. Someone else is in control of his life, just as it was in his childhood, and he is just trying to hold on as best he can. Time to climb back in the cockpit, Nick!

Should you discover yourself in a plane, find out in what direction you're flying. If it's upwards for take-off, you're moving towards greater enlightenment and awareness, whereas downwards and/or coming in for a landing can invoke many emotions—fear, excitement, dread, joy, obligation or true love. Your destination will give you clues as to what you can expect at the end of your flight of fancy; in Nick's case he was addressing a feeling of powerlessness he easily recognised from his childhood. The scenery will usually let you know what it is you need a birds-eye view of: are you flying over the water, inspecting your emotions? And don't forget to consider the shape and security of your dream plane and the reactions of your flight companions. Happy landings!

Ships

Ships and boats transport us from the shallow waters where we've temporarily docked, to the fathomless depths of our true feeling and stormy emotions. The type of vessel you require for your passionate dream voyages will indicate your need for either protection from your fear of intimacy, or the closer, smoother sailing of true love. Is your ship seaworthy, or have you found yourself slowly sinking into the mire of some emotional whirlpool of either obligation or true love? Do you know where your boat is heading, or is this just a preliminary sight-seeing tour of the riches that might lie in store for you? If you find yourself drifting in a dream boat, make sure you keep your life-jacket on—at least until you find a safe harbour for your heart's desires. If you're stranded, beached or sinking, search for where you are emotionally stuck in your waking life, and choose to resolve the emotional blocks that appear in your dreams.

A group of us are trying to get somewhere down a river on an outing. We're in a dinghy, but it keeps sinking. As it sinks, I find that I can easily pick it up and hold it out of the water and tip the water out. I'm proud of myself that I can do this, but every time I put it back into the water it sinks back. After several times of tipping the water out, I notice that a really fat lady keeps climbing into the boat from the rear, and she's making it sink. I figure that we need more than one boat to fit us all into. I go up on shore to get another boat.

I find myself in a house of sex, with the walls made out of woven cane—a temporary thing. It is a swinger's party, so I take off all my clothes, and as I walk past the reception desk there's an Asian man there who points to me and brings to my attention my underpants. I'm supposed to be naked. So I slip my underpants off, and then surprisingly I find I have a white loin cloth on underneath my underpants. I have to really pull to rip it off. Then I hear a loud-speaker calling to Mr Harry Edmonstone, which is my father's name. Since my father isn't here, I figure it's me they must be calling.

I go to the window, and a man there has a very small twin-hulled boat, which he offers to me to take my group further up the river. I say to him, 'This will be cheap to rent?', and he answers 'Two knots', thinking I'm asking how fast it will go. I finally get through to him that I want to know the price. He laughs and indicates it will be very cheap.

In this dream, Clive, of New South Wales, is a member of a social group on an outing. It's up to him to work out which particular 'group' the dream relates to—friends, family, work mates. They are all in a dinghy on the river, so we could safely say that this group is one which Clive has an emotional connection to in his waking life. They could even represent the many aspects of his own self. In the dream his boat is sinking—a sign he's getting swamped by his emotions, yet he's proud that he can keep it afloat, easily tipping the water out.

All water dreams show us symbols of our emotional journey. Perhaps in his waking life Clive feels proud of his ability to keep his emotional balance, controlling the degree to which he can surrender emotionally.

Clive becomes aware that the real cause of his problem is the fat lady who keeps climbing into the boat from the rear. What is the excess baggage this fat lady carries on board with her? Climbing in from the rear of the boat is a sign that she's probably someone he's taken on board at the last moment, or most recently. She could be someone he recognises, someone he thinks is excessive; or she may be symbolic of another strong feminine force in Clive's life, her bulk indicating the extent of the emotional weight she throws about in his dinghy. Either way, it's very clear the burden she's placing on him is making his emotional journey one of monotonous maintenance, with him doing all the work.

Rather than leave her behind, Clive figures he needs two boats, and goes ashore to find another one. He is certainly a responsible type, bravely coping with the sinking dinghy, wanting to accommodate everyone. In his quest to meet everyone's needs, he finds himself in a house of sex, where a swinger's party is taking place. What trouble he's having removing all his clothes—showing his true self! First he gets pulled up for still wearing underwear—ashamed to be free in his sexuality. Then when he removes the underwear, he remains protected by a loin cloth, suggesting he feels the need to project a very primitive, free and easy attitude with his masculinity and sexuality, perhaps to fit in with the perceived expectations of the group he finds himself with. Finally, when all the layers of his protection are removed, and he's available for physical and sexual intimacy, Clive is called over the loudspeaker by his father's name. This is a dream message alerting him to the fact that his sexuality is still influenced by his father, or his father's values.

After an initial bit of confusing and unclear communication, Clive finally gets the boat with the twin hull. However he would never have got the new boat if it wasn't for the fact that he was reminded of the negative 'calling' both he and his father have responded to. What is interesting is that when he finds his new boat, and haggles over the cost, the communication is initially confused, but eventually they 'speak the same language', there is laughter (joy), and Clive benefits by a cheaper price. This dream shows Clive two distinct issues: his emotional conflict with the 'fat lady' (a particular woman in his life) and his temporary escape to the sex house. The boat hire shows him that he is still paying for the fat lady, but by drawing on different resources within himself, other than his sexual 'front', he will be better equipped to keep both of them afloat.

Trains and Buses

Trains suggest we're sticking to conventional rails, both because they have a set route and time, and also because they carry many people along that particular line. Trains often move underground and through tunnels, so if you don't usually travel by train in your waking life, and you find yourself on a dream train, look at how you feel in society in general. Are you prepared to follow the line?

Faceless Extras

Imagine you are dreaming, and in your dream you find yourself aboard a sailing boat. Someone taps you on the shoulder, and you turn around to see one of the waiters standing there in a bow tie and nothing else, handing you a glass of sparkling Dom Perignon champagne. You blush, becoming suddenly aware of hundreds of vacationers sprawled out on deck chairs, their eyes fixed accusingly on your red cheeks. None of these people are familiar to you—in fact, you would be hard-pressed to accurately describe even one of them. But their presence is unmistakable.

The faceless extras are important dream characters representing society in general. When they appear as a sea of faces, ask yourself how you feel about them, and look at how they respond to you. The answer will reflect your world-view or how you believe others see you. Sometimes the significance of your dream characters will be easy to establish. More often, these famous or faceless personae tend to deliver messages that require some careful delving into; before you can uncover their significance in your waking life. For example, why do you just happen to be dreaming of that old primary school friend who you haven't seen in years, and not that *other* school friend you bumped into last week? And why is Steve Vizard the vampire attacking you and not the 'regular' Dracula?

Unprepared

Do you recall the gripping fear of walking into a dream exam for which you haven't studied, or of facing your dream boss who's impatiently waiting for the presentation you forgot to prepare? Why would you terrify yourself with such dream scenarios? Perhaps you have an abundance of guilt, fear and self-doubt, or even a heavy dose of low self-esteem to work through. With any luck these dreams will scare you enough to clear the cobwebs from your self-image and banish your unhealthy emotions.

'Unprepared' dreams are typical examples of how our fears and insecurities manifest themselves in our dream time, and are common to all of us at some time in our lives. A fear can be brought up by our daily activities and then magnified and re-enacted that very night, as we see in this next dream of Vicki's.

It was a few days before I ran a new course on psychic awareness, and I dreamt that the course had begun a week early. I was to give a preliminary lecture on the subject, but was completely unprepared. Whereas the actual course was to be attended by only six to eight participants, in my dream I was appearing before a crowd of a hundred people. When I finally found something to say, I became aware that hardly anyone was listening to me. The lecture theatre was in chaos, and quite a number of people had gone outside where they were swimming naked in the ocean. The police arrived and dragged them away. I felt like a miserable failure.

In this dream, Vicki was being warned that her self-doubt would manifest as failure in the up-coming course she was to run. Deep in her subconscious, Vicki doubted her ability to hold the attention of the participants and, more important, to safely control the real emotions that would surface in each participant during the course (portrayed by the students swimming nude), and felt she needed another authority figure to control the situation.

By Vicki experiencing this nightmare a few days before the course began, she had time to review her own attitude and resolve her insecurity. Incidentally, up to the time of having this dream, Vicki had very few people enrolled for the course. In the following week, after considering her dream and consciously acknowledging her fears, the number of students suddenly doubled. This is yet another example of how we influence our own circumstances, through our conscious and subconscious thoughts. Vicki's fears were acting as a block, hindering her from attracting students to the course. When she was able to resolve these blocks, she went on to create the attendance she really wanted. This is a perfect example of how our dream lessons can bring such positive effects into our waking life. We should be grateful that so many of our insecurities can be resolved in dream time, so that we're saved the embarrassment of having them manifest in our waking life.

Nightmares

Nightmares; those horrifying visitations we can't possible forget; those ghastly, gory scenes that leave us breathless and often paralysed with fear; images that linger beyond the fragments of the dream, frequently pursuing us into our waking lives; these dream messages are so powerful they absolutely insist we wake up and pay attention to them. The more tightly we have kept the lid on a belief, a feeling or a trauma, the wilder our nightmares will become. Horrible experiences that they are, you will have to admit that nightmares are very effective in alerting us to trouble in our subconscious self.

Is your primary dream-emotion anger, fear, sadness, hatred, rage, grief, guilt or resentment? Nightmares are, in fact, keeping you emotionally healthy. On a physical level, you may wake in a hot or cold sweat, or screaming in fright. Physical stress or suppressed anger can result in you grinding your teeth, loudly snoring or talking in your sleep. When you suppress too much sadness, you may wake up weeping. Mental nightmares are laced with confusion to the point that you wake up with a headache. During spiritual nightmares you can feel you won't ever discover the next step of your life purpose.

Naked Dreamers

These dreams show you 'the naked truth' about yourself and any areas of your real or imagined and most secret vulnerability. Depending on your age and the life issues you are currently facing, you may indeed literally be confronting your deepest fears of being caught in the nude. Again, depending on the context and contents of your dreams, you might find yourself in your dream time moving through a series of bizarre nightmares that will reflect any unconscious issues you have about your body.

Trauma Release Dreams

Deeply buried and traumatic emotions can also result in nightmares that will reveal to us all our fears and even some aspects of our emotional, nature which we have consciously repressed. These nightmares can, in some cases, be connected to deeply repressed traumas or childhood issues relating to either physical, sexual or emotional, mental or spiritual abuse. 'Selective memory' is how we effectively cope with surviving severe trauma. As adults, our negative beliefs, fears, concepts and the results of any unresolved traumas are especially damaging to our self-esteem and until we confront and resolve them, they can negatively affect all our personal relationships.

It's Back

Recurring dreams can indeed be seemingly endless nightmares to endure—they take you to the same scenes night after night, even in some cases, year after year; they can be very unsettling—and that is their purpose. Will you get the message as your dream moves you, yet again, towards its same inevitable conclusion? Perhaps you will continue to ignore it until the next time you re-run the same dream theme.

Other Interesting Dream Phenomena

Sleepwalking is not an uncommon occurrence, especially in our first seven years. Despite its prominence in movies, books and 'real life', very little is actually known about the phenomenon of sleep-walking. It is more common in children than adults, there are signs that it can be inherited, and it is often linked to emotional trauma. You would think that sleepwalking would link into the dream cycle, and could represent an acting out of dreams, however this appears not to be the case. It has been found that sleepwalking and sleep-talking occur in the non-REM sleep cycle (when there is no Rapid Eye Movement) and so may not coincide with dreaming at all!

Flying Dreams

If you're unsure whether your flying dream is an astral-travel experience or if it is merely symbolic, closely examine your feelings and the other events in the dream. In this way you'll soon discover where its meanings holds truth for you. Astral-travel dreams *feel* different from normal dreams. You may wake up with a sense that this was not an ordinary dream; you sense that you have actually been to some spot or met someone who is or will be special to you. Either way, a dream about flying is a great sign that you are rising to an elevated position in some area of your life!

Falling Dreams

A falling dream can also be symbolic and may have a number of meanings. It could imply 'taking the plunge' or making a commitment to something or someone in your life, 'slipping up' or 'falling down' means you may be off-track in what you're doing or it could even be a symbol of delving into the scary aspects of the issues in your life. The fast return of your astral body back into your physical body can sometimes manifest in your dreams as an experience like falling from a great height.

Past Lifetimes

Often the clues to past life-times come through your dreams. You may wake up knowing you have been speaking a foreign language in a dream; or see yourself wearing clothing that could only come from either a movie set or a memory of one of your past life-times. These are some of the ways past-life memories bleed through into present time.

You could actually be working out some past Karma with the dream characters in your present life, so it is vitally important when these types of dreams do occur to ask yourself, 'Who might this represent in my life now?' Use your intuition, and you may find that it's your father, Elton John, your boss, your current partner, your best friend, or the local butcher. However, just one dream like this is not always enough evidence of a past life. You will always get a very strong emotional reaction as well. It's either *déjà vu* or that 'ah ha' feeling! The dream scenario will give you greater insights into what the issues between you might have been, so that you are better equipped to deal with them effectively in this lifetime.

As souls, we all know everything about ourselves and when we take on our new physical bodies in each life-time, we move from the limitless, timeless spirit world, into the physical, limited, time zone of the material world, where we 'forget' our past experiences, bringing the essence of our talents and what is unresolved into our current birth script, as well as the traumatic events of our first seven years. Even if we never consciously consider our past realities, we can still carry these unresolved issues within us, as unconscious negative beliefs about ourselves.

Death and Dying

Because death is so often connected with suffering or violence, we fear it. We choose to be here (that's what free will is) out of individual choice. There are lots of dreams of death that are actually past life-time memories. The Irish saying 'I died a thousand deaths' is closer to the truth than we think—many of us have died more than a thousand deaths. We can when we use our free will with discrimination, realise that we are free to choose to focus on the negative aspects of our lives, or the positive ones.

Daily clearing

It has been shown that the content of our dreams in early periods of sleep is different from that of the dreams we have closer to waking. Our earlier dreams address many of the events and emotions from the previous day, and are believed to perform a type of 'daily clearing'. Often they assist us to release many of these feelings from our subconscious. This type of dream will tend to be much more jumbled, without following a clear storyline, and because they come from earlier in the night they are remembered less frequently than subsequent dreams. The daily clearing dreams often involve a partial replay of the situations of the day, and include some key characters from the dreamer's life. Thus, you may dream that you murder your boss after the argument you had that morning, or that you are searching and searching for your cat who disappeared that afternoon. Perhaps you are struggling again with the crossword puzzle you gave up on in the evening or, worse, you are being chased by the monster from the horror film you watched just before going to bed.

It has been suggested in experiments of sleep deprivation that it is this type of dreaming which is most needed by the body, and without which the body feels 'deprived'. This reinforces the idea that this daily clearing during our earlier dream periods is both beneficial and essential for our health and well-being, and may indeed be the brain's way of sorting the day's information and emotional responses before filing it away.

Astral Travelling

What if we are all astral-travelling every night and not dreaming at all? Indian yogis believe that we leave our bodies and that our spirit moves freely in the astral, or spirit dimension during sleep and also in some deep states of meditation or trance. The spirit is connected to the body by the 'silver cord', a kind of energy cord which allows us to leave our bodies and return again safely.

Death occurs when the silver cord that connects the spirit to the body is broken, and the spirit 'passes over' to the spirit dimension, leaving the physical body to return to the 'dust' of the earth. The presence of this energy or spirit within our bodies is confirmed by Kirlian photography, which shows the electromagnetic field or bio-electrical aura around all living things. At the time of death this area disappears, and the body becomes suddenly fractionally lighter, consistent with the departure of some 'life force' or energy. In plant life the aura fades slowly and the plant or fruit withers, and either dries or rots.

A large number of people have reported in near-death experiences the sensation of rising out of their physical body and looking down on resuscitation efforts, then suddenly finding themselves back in their body with their eyes open. Such an experience is a form of astral (or spirit) travelling, where we are conscious of other people, places or dimensions while our physical body is at rest, asleep, in meditation, or during an operation when we are drugged and unconscious.

In our daily lives we have all experienced astral travelling, leaving and returning to our bodies, although we may not always be consciously aware of what is happening. Many ordinary activities produce these out-of-body experiences (OBE) including orgasm, meditation, fasting and sleep.

Have you ever been asleep and woken with a start, feeling as if you have fallen from a great height? In actual fact, your body hasn't fallen, but your spirit has. It has rushed back to your body to deal with the interruption at hand. The shamans or medicine people of many cultures have developed conscious control over many of these out-of-body experiences, and utilise such travelling to heal the sick and move through other planes of existence.

Our ability to have out-of-body experiences also explains how we access knowledge from our dreams, such as prophetic warnings, and shared dreams. We move beyond the physical plane of exist-ence, and the limits of time where past, present and future events exist concurrently.

Australian Dreaming

Travel has broadened our perspectives, not only in a physical sense but also emotionally, mentally and spiritually. Many of us living in the mystical land of Australia have relatives and loved ones who live overseas. Many migrants dream of events occurring to their loved ones far away. Because Australia is an island and migrants generally have such strong ties with 'home', the psychic links began to occur, expanding from culture to culture as more and more people travelled and settled elsewhere. Global dreaming has been assisted by radio, movies, television, computers and now popular virtual reality systems. We all laugh and cry in the same language.

Each life is full of changes and transformations: from the first moment of our physical conception, we begin to change, in subtle and significant ways, and in each significant change, we embark on a new journey of self-discovery. Do any of us really know what potential lies within us as we evolve through time and personal experience—a potential to create something of exceptional beauty, or the need to soar to great heights and explore the mazes and amazes that lie within us?

It is through our dreams that we mostly access this inner knowledge and wisdom, dreams being the life-line that takes us into the deep unconscious and the intuitive subconscious part of ourselves, and back up to consciousness again. Dreams are an integral part of our life's journey. They are like a sacred mirror that reflects back to us our true self. Next time you look at yourself in the sacred mirror of your dreams, be aware, for in the depths of each and every one of us resides a unique and exceptional being, waiting only for the perfect moment when we discover our authentic self and get on with our unique life purpose.

The concept of the collective unconscious suggests that, on one level, we are all aware of everything that any other individual is aware of. Another way of looking at this collective awareness is the model of a global brain, in which all our individual brains are connected through a telepathic link. This is why we often say something that someone else was just about to say. It also explains why inventions and inspirations are so often shared.

Often it's an idea whose time has come, as the next logical step in a universal process, and frequently more than one person will have the same idea in a slightly different form. There is no copyright on the white-light of illumination. Life continually calls us forth to find individual completeness and personal fulfilment. Surely this is also true on a global level, where as human beings and inhabitants of this magnificent planet earth, we are moving towards unity as global citizens.

Changing the Course of History

Throughout the ages, dreams have dictated and directed the course of history. Dream prophecies and warnings are woven into many a biblical story, dream inspirations continue to appear in famous musical scores, countless paintings, plays, films and books.

The First Dream

To find the first human dream is almost an impossible task. Many animals dream—crocodiles, birds, all mammals. Yes, when your favourite tomcat is asleep and twitching, he *is* dreaming. But what is he dreaming about? Is he seeing himself courting the most desirable feline in the neighbourhood, or racing under hedges to avoid the neighbour's dog. With the progression up the evolutionary ladder, and the greater potential for problem-solving and forward-thought in primates and human beings, it is most likely that dreams have in turn become more complex. We can surmise that human beings have been dreaming since *Homo sapiens* first walked the earth, but no records of these early dreams exist; they were passed from generation to generation by word of mouth. The very first record of a dream dates back to Mesopotamian literature. It was a dream which predicted an impending disaster, a huge tidal wave that swamped much of the earth, surprisingly similar to the biblical account of the great flood in the time of Noah—what scientists know to be the end of the last ice age.

One of the oldest dream books still in existence was written in the second century AD. This encyclopedia, the Greek

Artemidorous's *Oneiro-Critica*, is a compilation of Assyrian, Egyptian and Babylonian dream-lore. Artemidorous used material from the library of the Babylonian King Asurnasi, and put forward the now-accepted theory that dreams are made up of a number of images, which, to be interpreted, should be considered in the context of their settings and the dream as a whole. He emphasised the importance of knowing the personality and life situation of the dreamer in interpreting dreams, even making the suggestion (later adopted by Freud) that many dream images have strong emotional and sexual elements. Since its writing, the *Oneiro-Critica* has been translated into English and reprinted more than 30 times. In fact, it dominated dream literature up to the nineteenth century, being the only significant book on the subject until that time.

Dreams from the Bible

One of the most substantial dream records from ancient times is the Bible. Many well-known dreams are nestled in its pages, dreams which were responsible for saving nations and guiding individuals.

Reports of dreams from both the Old and New Testaments, as well as other historical records from that time, are a clear reminder to us of the strong faith that was placed in dreams as a means of prophecy and guidance in many ancient societies. The biblical accounts of any dreams, including those dreamt by Joseph, are very straightforward to interpret. They are presented as literal messages, usually delivered by an 'angel of the Lord'.

Similarly, the ancient Greeks thought that Zeus, Father of the Gods, was responsible for sending them divine messages, aided by Hypnos, God of Sleep, and Morpheus, the God of Dreams.

To Know Your Future . . .

Many of us would be astonished to discover the influence of dreams on the lives of such famous people as Marie-Antoinette, Charles Dickens, William Shakespeare, Alexander the Great, Napoleon Bonapart and James Watt. Dreams have been elemental in directing the lives and inventions, creative output and destiny of the dreamers.

Wars have been won and lost as a result of dream inspirations. Almost 2,400 years ago Alexander the Great dreamed that a *satyr* (a natural spirit) danced on his shield. This dream came to him when Tyros was under siege, and his personal dream interpreter rearranged the letters in *satyros* to provide the message 'Tyros is thine'. This dream encouraged Alexander to continue his attack on Tyros with such confidence that Tyros surrendered almost immediately. Centuries later, Joan of Arc received powerful inspiration from her visionary day-dreams, and was motivated by a dream one night that showed she was destined to save France.

There are many recorded instances where dreams have contributed to military manoeuvres. Julius Caesar dreamed one night that he violated his own mother; soon after this dream he decided to take his army across the Rubicon, and thus 'invaded his motherland'. Napolean recorded his dreams each night, and used them to plan his military campaigns. These dreams he would act out, using toy soldiers to study each move and counter-move. Not many years later, in 1863, the German ruler dreamed that Prussia rose to power over the other German states. When this event actually happened, it was considered to be one of the causes of the First World War.

Among the more unfortunate precognitive dreams are those that predict death. Queen Marie-Antoinette while imprisoned by the French revolutionaries, dreamed of a glowing red sun rising above a column like a temple pillar. Suddenly the column cracked in half and fell to the ground—was this a prophecy of her beheading? US President Lincoln also saw his own death in a dream, and his body lying in state on a catafalque (raised platform). When he asked in the dream who had died, he was told 'The President is dead'.

Inventors' Paradise

Many inventions and new discoveries have also been inspired by dreams and visions. The inventor of the light bulb, Thomas Edison believed so strongly in dream inspiration that he would nap during working hours. He found that his dreams provided him with fresh ideas and solutions to his daily problems. James Watt discovered ball-bearings as the result of a recurring dream: in this dream he found himself walking through a rain of heavy lead pellets, over and over again. Finally he deduced that if he dropped molten lead from a great height, it would form into small spheres—ball-bearings. After realising this, the dream did not recur: he had finally 'got it'. Even the structure of the atom was discovered as a result of a dream image. Danish physicist Niehls Bohr dreamed of a sun made of burning gas, with planets spinning around it, attached by thin filaments. This dream encouraged him to conduct further research into atomic physics, which substantiated his vision of atomic structure.

An Influence on the Arts

'To sleep; /To sleep; perchance to dream: ay, there's the rub; /For in that sleep of death what dreams may come /When we have shuffled off this mortal coil /Must give us pause.'

With quotes such as this one gracing the pages of William Shakespeare's Hamlet, it's obvious that dreams have infiltrated our arts in many different forms. The dreaming nature, a series of wild images and fantasies, has provided the basis for many famous books and poems. Shakespeare's plays can be interpreted as if they were a string of dream images.

In a similar way Charlotte Brontë has used dream images to express the emotions of the little girl in her popular classic, *Jane Eyre*.

Lewis Carroll's exquisite *Alice in Wonderland* has for decades enthralled children with its fantasy world of mushrooms, white rabbits, nonsense verse, and the disappearing Cheshire cat. This story is, in fact, a very sophisticated expedition into the dreaming mind, revealing the fears and fantasies that dwell therein. Jules Verne's novels, *Twenty-thousand Leagues Under the Sea*, *Journey to the Centre of the Earth*, and *Around the World in Eighty Days* have indeed been prophetic. Perhaps a time machine will materialise at your nearest 'Time Zone' amusement arcade.

Dreams have inspired many famous literary works. They infused writer Graham Greene with the ideas for some of his plots, and have drifted into the poetry of both William Wordsworth and Robert Coleridge. Perhaps the best-known story inspired by a dream is Robert Louis Stevenson's *Dr Jekyll and Mr Hyde*, of which he wrote:

> *I had long been trying to write a story on this subject [of a double life], to find a body, a vehicle, for that strong sense of man's double being which must at times come upon and overwhelm the mind of every thinking creature. For two days I went about racking my brains for a plot and on the second night I dreamed a scene at the window, and the scene afterwards split in two, in which Hyde, pursued for some crime, took the powder and underwent the change in the presence of his pursuers:*

The purpose of dreams is to wake us up, to allow us to see ourselves as we really are, warts and all. Each dream we dream is an opportunity to resolve an emotional drama, solve a problem we face in life, or preview a probable future reality.

Each time you face your fears in a nightmare, it is an opportunity to empower yourself, step by step, dream by dream. When you reach the stage where you can turn to confront who or what terrorises you in your nightmare, you will begin to find new levels of courage in your waking life.

Solve the riddle of your recurring dreams and then move on to the next exciting aspect of self discovery. Above all, be patient with yourself as you decipher your dream messages, and learn to trust your insight and inner wisdom.

A a ... *Aspire to be carefree. Ask, and all ambitions will be realised. Your dreams will give you the courage to release yourself. They are but fleeting thoughts that can move you through all your unhealthy pain, allowing you to be truly authentic.*

Abandoned Left, rejected, lost and alone. A belief you are unwanted or unlovable.

Abasement Casting down or being cast down form a position of power to be either humbled or degraded. When you are 'put down' in your dream, it can be a warning; or you are dreaming your conscious or unconscious fears. When you abase another, you are trying to gain power in this relationship.

Abdomen The source of personal power, of 'gut feelings' and of personal identity. 'Butterflies in the stomach' are a sign of excitement, nervousness or your conscious or unconscious fears.

Abduction Can denote being out of control in a situation; carried away.

Aboriginal Elder; teacher; primitive law; spirit guide; someone you actually have seen, heard of or know in waking life.

Abortion Symbolically, it's aborting any personal project or relationship; losing a part of the self. If you have had or are contemplating an abortion in waking life, this dream may be allowing you to resolve some of your unconscious feelings about this decision.

Abreaction This release of tension resulting from a past unpleasant experience happens in dreams because we can more easily access and express unhealthy traumas of beliefs associated with forgotten events. This is also often accompanied by a time warp or by clues leading you to recognise timeframes relating to when this experience occurred in the past. It can also be the release from any complex or suppressed waking desire by acting it out in your dream.

Absence, absent Avoidance; not looking at some issue. Who is absent? What are you missing out on in your life? Withdrawn to a 'safe' distance to avoid looking at an issue; or dealing with someone difficult.

Accident May be precognitive of a real accident. If the dream accident occurs while you are in some form of transport, it indicates a change of direction occurring in your life—how you previously 'transported' yourself through life is no longer appropriate. If you run into something, you are going to fast. If something runs into you: you are in the wrong place at the wrong time; something needs to change. Accidents at sea relate to emotions or love affairs. See also **Crash.**

Accountant The responsible part of your self, to whom you must account for all your actions; your Higher Self; inner book-keeping; laws of Karma (cause and effect); could actually be an accountant in your waking life.

Acrobat Overcoming problems or dramas; to either leap or fall.

Actor Fantasies and ideals; the part of you who 'puts on an act'. The actor may also embody certain qualities which apply to you or someone around you. Find the qualities you attribute to this actor, and see how they apply in the context of your dream.

Adultery Cheating, unfaithfulness; guilt or desire; living out sexual fantasies in your dreams. Frequently it is showing you your own jealousy or possessiveness. It can also be an indication of your unconscious sibling rivalry, especially when you dream your beloved is cheating on you with close friends. Generally these dreams warn about something not in the best interests of all.

Aeroplane See **Flying Plane.**

Ageing Fear of the ageing process; yourself at a future age; experience or wisdom; future self.

AIDS As with any illness, you may be resolving your fears in your dream time.

Akashic record Your soul's Karmic history—everything you have ever thought, felt, done or experienced in this life-time or any other.

Alarm Pay attention!; beware, be aware; warning; fear; wakes you up to something you need to act on in your waking life.

Alcohol A drug or suppressant; alcohol suppresses fear; as such, it's an escape from reality; letting go of control; controlling others; loosening up; making a fool of yourself, depending on your dream content and actioning.

Alien An unfamiliar part of yourself or someone else; belief that you are 'different'; an actual extraterrestial.

Allergy Instantaneous repulsion. What issue are you avoiding in your life? Who are you allergic to? What are you angrily reacting to?

Alley In some dreams it can be a way you move back into your past; a short-cut; blind alley or dead end.

Amethyst Royal purple stone traditional bishop's ring; if worn on third finger of right hand signifies High Priest; protects from poisons.

Ammunition The words of knowledge that fuel a fight. Are you low on ammunition, feeling disempowered?

Amputation Loss of a part of yourself—'don't have a leg to stand on'.

Anchor Stabilising element; attachment; secure mooring.

Androgynous Being by nature both male and female; you are accessing the 49 per cent of you that is the opposite sex, to bring more balance into some area of your waking life.

Angel The angelic part of yourself; financial backer; Higher Self; Holy Spirit; spirit guide; a messenger from God.

Anger If anger comes up in your dream time, first look for this emotion within yourself. Use the dream scenario to give you clues as to how this applies in your own life, how you react to angry people around you; your need to release anger to ensure emotional fitness.

Anima If male, the 49 per cent of you that is female. When you dream of being female you are ignoring your feminine side; This also relates to the left side of your body and your right-brain functions, such as intuition and intimacy; your ability to receive things, thoughts and feelings from others, especially love and support.

Animal A symbol of your instinctual emotions and reactions;

may also refer to your concerns about an animal in your waking life. Examine what qualities you believe the animal embodies, draw on its strength, and look for what it may be telling you about yourself; also the specific animal's nature.

Animus If female, the 49 per cent of you that is male. When you dream of being male you are ignoring your male side; this also relates to your left-brain and the right side of your body; inspirational, competent, creative and active, especially adding value to something or someone.

Ankh A tau cross with a loop on top. An ancient Egyptian symbol or emblem of eternal life; immortality; prosperity.

Ankle Are you feeling unsupported, inflexible, or resisting change in your waking life?

Anorexia Starving yourself emotionally or spiritually; total control of one's body as a protest against feeling controlled by others; lack of emotional nourishment and nurturing; this can be giving you dietary advice or a warning.

Ants Depending on the context of your dream, can be irritations; industry; cooperation; society.

Anus Negative: fear of letting go; keeping tight control; pent-up emotions. Positive: release; relaxed; expressed; can be sexual in some dreams.

Apartment A place apart; aloneness; if you live in this apartment in waking life, it may not be symbolic.

Apathy Not feeling, insensitive to the feelings of others; living a passionless existence; these dreams help you to wake up to yourself and decide what action to take.

Applause A form of encouragement, congratulations on an achievement.

Apple Nourishment; health; desire and/or temptation; trying to please someone.

Aquamarine Said to endow the wearer with courage; stability and focus; used in the seventeenth century in times of war.

Archetype An inherited idea or mode of thought, derived from the experience of the race and present in the unconscious of the individual, controlling his ways of perceiving the world.

Architect May be someone you actually know; the 'architect' in your life who 'makes things happen'; the designing part of yourself; higher designs; Higher Self.

Architecture The style (eg. Gothic, renaissance, neo-classical) indicates a time-frame; can often indicate the historical period when a past life occurred.

Arena The stage of life; sports arena; is it time for a change of event?

Argument As in waking life, any conflict, or heated or passionate exchanges. Often arguments in dreams help to keep you emotionally fit. Occasionally, it may be prophetic and warn you to avoid an argument.

Armour Rigidity; defensive; self-protective; unfeeling; you may need a tin-opener.

Arms Issues to do with giving and receiving support, or giving and receiving intimacy in relationships.

Army Overpowering opposition; a battle to *win*. See also **War**.

Arrested Unlawful; the halt to a project or idea; arrested development.

Arrow Aiming for a goal or target in your life; aggression, sport. See also **Dart**.

Ashes What remains of yourself, your goals, your love or some other aspect of your life once it has 'burned out'; any issues around death or depression (remember the phoenix whose rebirth comes through fire); new beginnings. See also **Dust, Birth, Death**.

Astral travel You may actually be astral travelling, we all do: while your body is in a deep trance or asleep, your spirit travels to meet with your Higher Self, loved ones who are far away or even those who have passed on to other dimensions.

Athlete Physical ability; running from life or from facing issues.

Attack Conflict. How are you feeling attacked in your life? Are you the aggressor or the victim? Do you fight back or run and hide? These dreams help you to confront your fears when you are the victim, or to release your rage when you are the attacker.

Attic A house is always a symbol of yourself, each room reflecting an aspect of you: the attic represents higher consciousness; higher thought; any aspect of your physical, emotional, mental or spiritual attainment.

Audience Hearing the many parts of yourself; the many players in your life; may be a message to 'hear' the words you speak and 'watch' your own actions.

Authority Those in power; those 'in the know'; Higher Self or inner authority.

Autumn Fulfilment, fruition; gathering stores, taking stock.

Avalanche Things are moving too fast in your life, threatening to overwhelm you, sweep you away or crush you.

Award Congratulations on your success in something; a grant or prize.

Axe Conflict; cutting to the truth; danger. What needs to be hacked out, hacked about, hacked off or at least re-ordered in your life? A Norse symbol.

B b ... Begin by not judging what you see. Each dream is an introspection bringing to birth a part of you too shy to reveal its face in the light of day. Dreams are born of sensitivities that may or may not still serve you well. Be businesslike.

Baby New beginning; new idea; new project; may refer literally to your child if you have one, or to your own childhood; your own infantile emotions.

Back What is 'behind' you, the past; subconscious thought; past issues; hidden areas; Karma or the laws of cause and effect; a retrospective lack of awareness.

Backseat Moving through life without being in control. Whose vehicle are you in? Who is in the driver's seat?

Backyard Unconscious; back of mind; back brain, primitive instinctive brain; literally, what's going on in your own backyard. See also **Garden**.

Bags Emotional baggage; as 'old bags' or wizened hags.

Bait How are you being lured in your life, or is it you doing the luring?; 'jailbait'—person under the age of sexual consent; any temptation.

Baking The gestation period of a new idea or project. What are you cooking up? 'A bun in the oven'—you are pregnant. Nurturing and sharing especially if you love to cook; chefs frequently dream up new recipes.

Balcony Wider perspective in life; in a position to see the world around you.

Bald Lack of personal power; bare, as in 'bald lie'. See also **Hair**.

Ball A symbol of childhood; fun and games; debut; a gala celebration; to 'have a ball', have a great time; 'to ball' safely you need a condom.

Balloon Expanded consciousness; beyond the physical; fun; a symbol of childhood and celebration; moving to a higher understanding; feeling easily deflated; elevating feelings; floating; playing; conversation balloon in cartoons.

Balls Gonads; testes; courage; macho power. See also **Scrotum**.

Bandage Immobilising or restraining a part of yourself; supporting a hurt.

Bandaid Trying to patch things up; a temporary solution to your problem.

Bandit See **Burglar**.

Bank A symbol of wealth, credit and debts; certainty—'you can bank on it!'

Banquet Feast on; it can indicate your suppressed need for love or nurturing or a warning about your gluttonous indulgences.

Bar Barrier; restricted options; ban; singles bar. See also **Pub**.

Barbecue Socialising; friendship; fun; nourishment.

Barricade Barrier to the self; goals difficult to achieve.

Barrister See **Solicitor**.

Basement An aspect of self; often the lowest levels of your soul accessed via your subconscious mind; often where you find childhood memories or traumatic events that need release in your life now.

Basket Symbol of the feminine; skills or accessories you carry around to complement your own abilities; if a picnic basket, may symbolise relaxation, romance and adventure; 'a basket-case'—needs professional help.

Bat Genetic memories; attuned perceptions; ability to navigate through life's dramas; a love of the dark, the hidden and the mysteries of life; 'bats in the belfry'—crazy. If it scares you, it's negative; if not, it's positive. See also **Vampire**.

Bath, bathing Cleansing; refreshing; 'clean up' a problem in your life.

Bathroom An aspect of self-cleansing, elimination; beautifying.

Battery Life energy, 'aliveness'; you probably need re-energising.

Battle Opposing ideals; inner conflicts. See also **Enemy**.

Beach The point where the material (earth) meets the emotional (water). It's the natural part of yourself and because

Australia is an island, we all frequently dream of beaches. It relates to your emotions and to putting your feelings into action in the physical world. Don't just think about it, dive in!

Bear Grumpy nature, as in 'bear with a sore head'; lovable and loving as a teddy bear, or in 'a bear hug'; grizzly bear—potential for harm; can symbolise a fear of society.

Beard Ancient wisdom; covering up the true self.

Bed bedroom Sex, sexual issues; rest and recuperation.

Beer Escape from reality. See also **Alcohol, Drugs**.

Bees Activity—'busy bees', 'buzzing around,' loyalty; 'stinging' comments; getting 'stung' on a deal; 'hive of industry'; cooperation.

Beg Pleading, needy; dependent; 'beggars can't be choosers'.

Bell You are being alerted to something; time to take action now; can be prophetic if wedding bells; or just your fantasy, depends on the context of your dream and waking life.

Belt Restraint; discipline; be quiet, as in 'belt up!'; 'below the belt'—what passion is hiding beneath your belt?

Betrayal May be actual betrayal; who or what don't you trust in your life? Can also relate to an unconscious fear that may be based on unresolved childhood sibling rivalry issues.

Bible Book of wisdom; religious gospels; conventional word of God.

Bicycle Balance, activity, mode of transport for children and teenagers.

Bill Time to pay for your actions; . See also **Cost, Karma**.

Birds Freedom; spirit; messengers of the Gods; can signify telepathy. See also individual birds, such as **Crow, Eagle**.

Birth The Self reborn; fear and pain, or joy and bliss; new ideas; birth of a new project; at times of major change in life you might dream your birth-script, the unconscious memory of your actual birth—you might find yourself in a symbolic tunnel or an undulating landscape.

Bisexuality Living out taboos, fears and secret fantasies in dreams; expressing both the male and female sides of yourself sexually.

Bite, bitten Feeling attacked; a 'love bite'; outward manifestation of inner anger.

Black Absorbs all colours; protection; completions and endings; 'in a black mood'—depressed; the unknown. See also **Dark, Night**.

Blade Pioneering, as in the 'cutting edge' of life; attack; potentially dangerous, depending on who wields the dream blade.

Blanket Of security; secrecy; togetherness; a symbol of protection especially in children's dreams. See also **Quilt**.

Blessing The grace of God; a gift or ability; a boon; approval.

Blind Can't see; avoiding seeing something; a 'blind spot'; 'blind drunk'.

Blindfold Unable to see what's going on; why is it there? The dream action will give you clues about what you are prevented from seeing in your waking life.

Blister Rubbed the wrong way—irritation; overuse; a sign of anger; can be a sign or manifestation of blistering heat or metaphoric anger.

Blood Life force, deeply wounded; blood on hands—guilt.

Blossom New opportunities; new growth; an opening of yourself towards others and life.

Blue Creativity; self-expression; intuitive perception; trust; contemplation and peace; 'blue', sad and depressed; 'black and blue'—covered in bruises; 'blue' jokes, movies magazines—pornography; hope, as 'blue skies'.

Boat Symbolises how you move through life emotionally; in touch with your emotions; 'missing the boat', or 'full steam ahead'; it can actually be your boat.

Body The temple of the soul.

Bomb Something is about to detonate in your life; a symbol of failure, as in 'it's a bomb'. See also **Explosion**.

Bondage Feeling confined and restricted; sexual fantasies. See also **Abasement**.

Bone Support; structure; a sign of deep emotional injury, as in 'cut to the bone', 'I feel it in my bones'—a deep feeling or premonition.

Book Message; past learning or Karma; knowledge; a detailed lesson.

Boomerang Something coming back to you; a fast return.

Boot To end something, as in 'give it the boot', kit it out; walking.

Borrow To seek a loan.

Boss May refer literally to your boss; your parents; your Higher Self. See also **Chief**.

Bottle Something bottled up; something kept or preserved.

Bound Feeling restricted; commitment, as in 'bound to a promise'; fate, as in 'bound to happen'.

Box Feeling restricted, 'boxed in'; 'box', vagina—a sign of the feminine; the womb; something 'out of the box'—special or expensive; 'jack in the box'—surprise! What is in the box?

Boy The boyish side of yourself; may symbolise a boy you know; if female, your animus or the 49 per cent of you that is male.

Boyfriend May literally be your boyfriend; sign of friendship and love; feeling close to the male part of yourself.

Brain Thought, both conscious and subconscious; physical, emotional, mental and spiritual intelligence.

Brake Stopping if out of control, 'put the brakes on'.

Branch Reach out; branch out; explore other options.

Bread Money; food, as in 'bread on the table'; 'breadline'—sign of poverty and humility.

Break Smash; fracture; break up; need to 'take a break'; 'break out', escape; 'break down' into each component; emotional or nervous 'breakdown'.

Breast Nurturing; motherhood; caring; milk of human kindness.

Breath The breath of life; life energy; life force; will to live; an indicator of emotional states: passion, love, anger, sadness, fear, joy.

Bricks Building blocks of life; barrier; stubborn or dim-witted, as in 'thick as a brick'; security, as 'behind brick walls'.

Bridge Bridging a gap; forming a link; joining; connecting people or things; a vital clue if your 'bridge' is falling down.

Briefcase A symbol of business; tools for work; a 'brief case history'. What information or secrets do you carry around with you? See also **Luggage**.

Broke See **Poverty**.

Broken Something's not working in your life. See also **Break**.

Broom Time to sweep out the rubbish in your life, the patterns that no longer serve you; inner spring-cleaning.

Brother Could, literally, represent your brother; also 'brother-hood of man', friendship and humanity.

Brown The colour of earth, soil which gives life; also the colour of mud, suggesting a lack of clarity; hidden identity; worn by members of religious orders.

Building Like houses, a symbol of the working self, or your work self-image; When you own the building it is not symbolic.

Bull Lies, as in 'bull-shit'; rage; stubborn, as in 'bull-headed', eager, as in 'like a bull to a gate', insensitive; fiery or sexual energy.

Bulldozer Pressure to have own way; 'bulldozing' ideas through; 'dredging up' issues.

Bullseye Your exact goal; aim; objective; 'hit the bullseye'—hit the mark.

Burglar Feeling threatened; someone is stealing something from you; may also be a prophetic warning. What are you most afraid to lose?

Burn Sign of anger; burning with unconscious rage; a 'burning issue'. See also **Fire**.

Burrow Family connections; social organisation; a part of the self which is buried from view; the subconscious mind. What are you hiding from yourself?

Bus Travelling the scenic or pedestrian route in your life; mode of transport for old people, school kids and workers; if you don't normally travel by bus, it may be a time warp dream to a time in your life when you did so.

Bush Natural self; instincts; down-to-earth; earthy pursuits.

Butterfly The soul and its transformation; beauty and freedom; a fickle nature, fluttering from idea to idea, partner to partner; or a 'social butterfly'. See also **Moth**.

Buttocks The seat of the problem; an area requiring discipline in your life; sex and sensuality.

C *c* ... *Celebrate your every dream character. They are a component of you made larger than life to help you see yourself more clearly. Have a good chuckle at your own creative landscapes and yourself. Release the past so you find your natural state of joy and freedom.*

Cabinet See **Cupboard**.

Café Your social life; issues around nurturing, nourishment and food.

Cage Trapped; kept for observation or on display, as in a zoo.

Cake Your goal; a product or invention; gluttony; celebration; special treat; 'icing on the cake'—extra enjoyment, the sweetest part.

Calculator 'Calculating', taking account of your actions; weigh up your gains and losses; time to put the pieces together.

Calendar Time for something to happen; a project; cycles of life; 'flow charts'; relates to your time lines or deadlines in your school work, business or home life.

Camera Visual record of what you are doing now, for later recall; memories.

Camping 'Roughing it', at one with natural surroundings; fun with friends and family; exploring unfamiliar territory within and without.

Cancer Something has taken over your life; an obsession, growing out of control; unexpressed rage and resentment; self-loathing; feeling unlovable. If you have cancer in your waking life, you may be resolving your fears in your dream time.

Candle Lighting the way for your next steps; illumination; purification; 'votive candles', or these set alight in remembrance of the dead.

Cane Pointing the way; something which can lead you through the areas of life to which you are blind; discipline needed in your life.

Cannot move Forced to watch your deepest fears. What beliefs and fears prevent you from moving or acting in your life? See also **Paralysed**.

Canoe Travelling through life in close contact with your emotions; potential instability; manoeuvrability.

Captain The part of you in charge of your life, 'your own ship', your direction and your emotions; someone to whom you hand over control in your life; Higher Self; literally, you, if you own a boat.

Car Personal direction; movement in life; symbol of your body. Are you in the front seat or the back seat? Who is steering this car? Whose car is it?

Carpenter The part of yourself that can put ideas together; making something of your life; may refer to a carpenter you know in your waking life.

Carpet Protection, as in something that's 'swept under the carpet'; the secret, unspoken foundation of the problem; warning not to 'pull the rug out from under you'; comfort and homeliness.

Castle Family history; earlier generations; the ancient part of the self.

Castrate To lose your courage, your 'balls' your masculinity or manhood.

Cat Catty; a well-fed cat will play with its prey; sensual; sexual instincts; feminine; curiosity; aloof; mysterious; cats are said to be telepathic and psychic; a dislike of cats can be jealousy or a possessive and controlling nature, as cats can only be wooed, never controlled. See also **Pet**.

Caught Something you've been avoiding has caught up with you; time to take responsibility for your emotions and your actions.

Cave Unconscious mind; in some dream scenarios it can symbolise a womb or a desire for hibernation; something secret and hidden. Can also be the primitive part of the self, or a past-life memory.

Ceiling Reached the limit; a protection; low ceilings, feeling restrained—no space; high ceilings, higher thoughts and feelings. You may find yourself floating up to the ceiling as you astral-travel.

Celibacy Time to review your sexual issues and sexual needs. Acknowledging these needs. Is it better to channel your sexual energy into other vital areas of your life?

Cell The prison inside of you; feeling trapped by your guilt, shame and blame; life's partitions; aloneness, isolation or separation.

Cellar Aspect of self (see **Basement**). Also, literally, a wine cellar.

Ceremony A celebration; graduation; ritual; a symbol of you attaining a rite of passage, something it's time to move through in waking life. See also **Initiation**.

Chair Support; pause or 'take a seat', 'sit' on your problem; chair a meeting; chairperson of the board; your position in life.

Champagne. Escape from reality. See also **Alcohol**.

Channel Narrow options, particularly emotionally; narrow viewpoint; energy being channelled in one direction; 'go through the right channels'; to 'channel' a spirit guide, allow another to speak through you for a short time.

Chase Something you're denying or have forgotten is catching you up; fear of being caught or trapped. What part of yourself, your fears or your actions, are you running away from?

Cheap Poor-quality, 'cheap and nasty', bad taste; a good deal; 'get it cheap', won't 'cost' you much in your life, won't require much sacrifice; 'Cheap woman'—a tart; 'he's cheap'—meaning with his money.

Cheeks Blushing; unconscious shame and deep embarrassment.

Cheese Nourishment; dietary advice; not feeling well, as in 'feeling cheesy'.

Chess The game of life; setting yourself up against an opponent.

Chest Pride; self-esteem; area of the heart; lungs; breast, heart chakra (energy centre).

Chew Taken on too much, as in 'bitten off more than you can chew', mulling over something, as in 'chew it over'. See also **Teeth**.

Chicken Lacking courage, 'you chicken'; are you suffering the effects of battery hen existence, being forced into society's mould?

Chief Someone in charge, leader of the tribe; police chief; chief of staff; a wise teacher, or elder. See also **Boss**.

Child Your inner child; your own childhood or your child-like qualities of trust, wonder, enthusiasm and joy; may also, literally, be a child you know.

Childhood Generally suggests a time warp, warning you that there is an unconscious, unresolved issue to understand, forgive and release.

Chocolates Special treat; gluttony; celebration; romance; a chocolate addict; a present or gift.

Choir Voices rise and fall in harmony; messages from above, an angelic choir; spiritual chanting; fellowship with others, singing songs of gratitude, to praise God.

Choking Difficulty accepting something; choking on unexpected emotions. What can't you swallow? If someone is choking you, what are they stopping you from expressing?

Church Place of worship; the spiritual, ritual or religious side of yourself.

Cigarettes A means of escaping from feeling your emotions, especially suppressing anger, a calming influence or taking a break.

Circle, circular Wholeness; completeness; a symbol of spirit. See also **Ring, Mandala**.

Circus Don't take it seriously; have fun; putting on an act.

City Symbol of society and power; the business districts.

Clam Not speaking the truth, as in 'clamming up'; the part of you that lies on the bed of your emotions; 'tight as a clam'.

Class Learning an important lesson.

Classroom The studious part of yourself; may be an astral instruction.

Claw Defence; viciousness; attack; 'claw your way out'.

Clean Awareness in a particular area; not allowing emotional rubbish to build up; goodness; a 'clean' mind. See also **Broom**.

Cleaner The part of yourself or someone else who helps to clean out your old outmoded habits and behaviours; may, literally, be someone you know who works as a cleaner.

Cleaning Cleaning out your old beliefs and patterns.

Cliff Stepping into the unknown; new adventures; a precipitous situation.

Climb Rising to a higher understanding in your life; climbing the career ladder; spiritually moving to higher levels or spiritual planes. See also **Mountain, Stairs**.

Clock Running out of time; your personal timing; a time issue is involved.

Clone Reproduce from a cell of living tissue; a copy of someone or something.

Clothes Your attitudes; the image you project; style, an aspect of your self-expression.

Clothesline Domestic instincts; time to air out old habits; hanging something out in full view, as dirty washing or your personal or intimate problems.

Cloud If dark, a problem hanging over your life; any oppressive feelings or bouts of depression; what has clouded your true vision or dimmed your unique perspective; look for the silver lining or the positive value of this problem; 'not a cloud in the sky'—a bright outlook.

Clown Acting the fool; making light of some problem; clowning around; having fun; are you the 'clown' or is someone else?

Club Meeting place; society; social club; weapon; suit of clubs in playing cards, suit of wands, rods or staffs in Tarot cards.

Coat Attitudes; how you present yourself to the world. See also **Overcoat**.

Cobwebs Old beliefs and patterns; something you haven't looked at in a long time; ancient; antique; 'clear away the cobwebs'.

Coccyx Or tailbone, is the site of your Kundalini energy, what the Indian yogis call 'the sleeping serpent'; symbolises energy and aliveness, your goals, aspirations and desires.

Cockatoo Making a loud 'noise' or commotion about something; being heard; an intelligent talking bird. See also **Birds**.

Coffee Stimulant; feeding anger; take a break; socialising—meeting for coffee.

Coffin Relates to any issues you have around death, it can sometimes be prophetic and mean someone you know is ready to leave the planet. When you dream of a coffin, don't panic—usually it's an old aspect of yourself that is dying.

Coins Small rewards; can be 'change' is coming your way; corresponds to the suit of Diamonds in playing cards—Coins being the suit of Diamonds in Tarot cards. See also **Money**.

Cold Fear isolation as in 'out in the cold'; being 'cold' towards other people; aloof. See also **Frozen**.

Collar Attachment; being led around; barrier to speech and expression.

Colours Colours influence us emotionally and can be significant in our dreams. People who mostly dream in technicolour will find a black and white dream significant; others who dream mostly in black and white will find a dream in colour more significant. In general, your preferences for various colours may influence your dreams. See also individual colours, **Blue, Green etc**.

Comet A symbol of awareness; a spiritual sign; enormous energy. See also **Shooting star**.

Compass Issues around your personal direction; which way to go? Wholeness , as in 'encompassing every point'.

Computer Work; 'computing' or integrating your own thoughts and beliefs; inner organisation; rational, logical and mental order, especially memory.

Concrete A good foundation; something solid; fixed, as 'set in concrete'.

Conditioner Nourishment for the hair; conditioning the self; richness and strength; beauty.

Condom Play it safe sexually; a safe barrier; protection from unwanted disease or pregnancy.

Confession It's time to tell the truth; spiritual confession and atonement.

Constipation Holding on to old patterns; literally, you may be scared 'shitless'.

Container Symbol of the feminine; may be containing your own powers or potential.

Contraceptive Prevention; a barrier to conception; play it safe.

Convention Conventional; as a forum for meeting like minds or sharing ideas.

Convict Can relate to convict-consciousness, the Australian 'cultural cringe', feeling 'less than' others. See also **Criminal**.

Cook, cooking The part of you who 'cooks up' new ideas, and nourishes the self. (What are you cooking up?) Preparation of food; nourishing others.

Copper Flexible, a conductor of electricity; known to alleviate arthritis; aiding 'flexibility.'

Corpse Cut off from a part of yourself; some part of you has died; a lack of feeling or energy and aliveness; a symbol of death, although not usually prophetic. See also **Coffin**.

Corrosion Wears away; destroyed; decay; something eating away. See also **Rust**.

Cost Symbol of the 'cost' of something to yourself, not always money, but in terms of personal sacrifice—as either time, energy or kindness. See also **Bill**.

Costume Often denotes a past-life connection, the many roles you play; how you present yourself to the world.

Cot A time warp to childhood; child-like cage; unfulfilled needs for security, attention and nurturing.

Counsellor Your inner counsel or your Higher Self, unless other influences indicate a need for professional help.

Course Race course; the course of life, life path; 'to run the course'—a race or lesson in your life; onward movement; course of a meal—first, second course.

Court Judging something; weighing up the good and the bad.

Cow Being inappropriate, as in 'silly cow', slow-thinking; contented; maternal; nurturing, as in 'milk for the masses'.

Crab As a sideways movement; an alternative perspective; being argumentative and 'crabby'; crabs, a particularly nasty form of sexually transmitted lice (*Pediculus pubis*).

Cradle Issues around nurturing, love and safety; time warp to childhood.

Crash Fall; come crashing down. See also **Accident**.

Cream Bonus, as in 'the cream on top'; best, as 'the cream of the crop'; luxury; decadence; sexual attraction, as in 'creaming her jeans'.

Creature A created thing; animal, as distinct from humans; 'creature comforts'; 'the creature' or whisky—hence 'the demon drink'. See also **Monster**.

Criminal A dangerous person; illegal action; beyond society's rules and boundaries; can indicate a warning or danger. See also **Prisoner**.

Crocodile 'Crocodile tears'—immersed in emotions that are not true feelings; predatory and reptilian instincts.

Cross Used for crucifixion, a symbol of Christianity; 'on the cross'—a martyr; cross one's self as a sign of protection; draw a line across as in 'cross out, off', 'cross a cheque'; go across a road, river, sea; cross paths, 'star-crossed lovers'; 'crosspatch'—bad-natured person; 'cross-breed'—racially mixed; to 'cross-reference' from one part of book to another.

Cross-dressing Exploring the other side of yourself, either male or female; may be living out a fantasy through your dreams.

Crossroads Indecision; a choice; which way to go?

Crow Crow of a rooster; a warning; old and pedantic, as in 'the old crow', 'crows feet' wrinkles around the eyes; watchful; raucous; carrion scavengers; 'as the crow flies'—straight. See also **Birds**.

Crutches Your 'crutches' in life, things you may be dependent on; unhealthy dependencies, addictions or how you use drugs to escape from reality.

Crying Crying or calling out for someone or something; your conscious or unconscious inner sadness.

Crystal ball Consider your future; may indicate a prophetic dream; clear-seeing psychic skills and intuition.

Cult System of religious worship often following unconventional lines; any secret society; limiting yourself to one truth; following without question.

Cup Symbol of love and fulfilment—'loving cup', prize for a race etc.; corresponds to the suit of Hearts in playing cards, Cups being the suit of Hearts in Tarot cards.

Cupboard Symbol of the feminine; hidden parts of the self.

Current Time, belief or practice; in general circulation, 'go with the flow'; strong direction; following the same events, current affairs; electrical current.

Curtain Privacy; protection; not showing self to outsiders.

Cushion Comfort; protection; 'cushioning' the impact of something.

Cut Divide; shorten; 'cut off', ignore; 'cut out', 'cutting' to the truth; cutting ties; 'cutting' remarks—wound or attack. See also **Injury**.

Cutlery Tools for eating; life's tools; how you nourish yourself.

Cyclone This is a warning things are building up; perhaps it's a wild vortex of violent emotions about to be unleashed either on you or by you.

Dd ... *Discriminate between that which is truly you and that which you have adopted or unconsciously conform to. The invader in your dreams is what you have taken on board, that could now be discarded. Be diligent in this, be discerning.*

Dam Symbolises a dammed-up reservoir, especially your blocked or held-back emotions.

Dance 'The dance of life', move with rhythmical steps; sacred dance; a celebration; sensuality; in touch with your body; social events; ritual dance.

Danger Generally a warning to wake up or be aware; if such dreams recur, they can be prophetic.

Dark Unilluminated; without light; the unconscious; subconscious; as in 'in the dark', can't see; night; the 'dark side', as evil; the hidden; the unenlightened. See also **Black**.

Dart Any pointed missile; fast or scattered energy, as in 'darting about', 'darting here and there'; a pointed attack; finding direction in your life; a singular goal, as in 'bullseye'. See also **Arrow**.

Daughter May literally be your daughter; if female the young girl is a part of you; if male, your anima.

Dawn Starting afresh; the beginning of a project, idea; a new beginning.

Daylight, daytime More light on the subject; conscious; illuminated; enlightened.

Deaf Unable to hear what's being said; blockage of auditory ability; who or what don't you want to listen to any more? What are you avoiding hearing?

Deal 'Good deal', large amount; 'deal with', cope; deal cards; business deal; dealer or trader.

Death Change; death of the old form, birth of the new form, rebirth; relates to personal issues around death. The death of a parent is often a symbol of their influence over you dying, or of the death of a situation, rather than their actual death.

Debt Something owing in your life; 'a debt of gratitude', being in someone's debt.

Deep Into the depths of your being, or your subconscious; deep emotions.

Defecate Letting go of unwanted patterns and accumulated physical waste; can also in some dream scenarios be a time warp to toilet training or unconscious fears of body functions.

Demon Supernatural being, inferior deity, evil spirit or ghost, cruel malicious minion or slave of the Devil. See also **Devil, Monster**.

Dentist Teeth; decisions; the part of you responsible for making decisions; may, literally, be a need to see a dentist.

Desert A barren or unexplored part of yourself; devoid of emotions.

Desk Symbol of work and study.

Detective Become a detective to yourself; investigate some aspect of your life.

Devil The parts of yourself you want to deny; bad; evil intentions; debauchery and lust; temptation; the forbidden. See also **Demon**.

Dew A life-sustaining force; always fresh; nurturing especially the emotions.

Diamond The gem within; diamond-fire; something you value; a girl's best friend. Considered the most valuable of all gems. Can mean cold and hard, thus giving clarity; relates to willpower; also amplifies the essence of other stones; suit of Diamonds in playing cards or suit of Stones or Coins in Tarot cards.

Diarrhoea Letting go of all your 'shit', those unwanted patterns; 'shit-scared'.

Dice Taking a gamble in life; cut into cubes, as in diced vegetables.

Dig Dig down into the subconscious; dig up old memories; enjoyment, as in 'dig it' or get into it.

Dinghy A symbol of how you journey through your emotional life, in touch with your emotions, but easily immersed in them.

How precarious is your situation? Are you full of hot air?

Dingo The wild, aggressive, masculine side of yourself; in Australia, baby-snatcher. See also **Dog**.

Dining room Issues around food, family and friendship, especially communication, entertainment and sharing; family and friendship.

Dinner Nourishment; nurturing; your social self; prelude to intimacy.

Dinosaur Hidden, suppressed; new ideas from ancient wisdom.

Dirt, dirty Something needs cleaning up in your life; 'dirty-minded'; your judgments on 'good' and 'bad'; any unpleasant characteristic. See also **Dust**.

Disease A physical manifestation of a spiritual, emotional or mental issue, as illness or disease.

Ditch 'Ditched', got rid of, thrown away. See also **Hole**.

Dive Taking the plunge; diving down into your emotions or your subconscious; getting closer to the truth; things not going well, as in 'life's taking a dive'.

Divorce Division; separation; break-up; may be either prophetic or a warning to act on resolving an issue or lack of intimacy.

Dizzy Too much activity; sick of going around and around in circles; silly; dizzying heights.

Doctor Healer; healing influence; health authority figure; seeking a cure.

Dog Domesticated instincts; loyalty; 'man's best friend'; savage instincts; 'treated like a dog', or treated badly. See also **Dingo**, **Pet**.

Doll Okay in children's dreams; in adults' dreams, fear of control.

Dolphin The part of yourself that is sensual or immersed in your emotions; joy; protection; leadership; family; synchronicity (perfect timing).

Donkey Stubbornness; stupidity; 'plodding' through life; bearing burdens.

Doors The way out and the way in; closed, barriers; open, opportunities.

Dope To drug, as in 'dope a horse'; marijuana or 'dope'; a stupid person.

Dough A play on words for 'money' and 'need'.

Doughnut See **Circle**.

Dove A spiritual messenger of peace and hope; a holy spirit. See also **Birds**.

Down Heading down into the subconscious; down into the emotions; a pessimistic outlook, as in life is going 'downhill' or feeling 'down', 'down and out'.

Dracula Vampire; someone taking advantage of you, 'sucking you dry'. See also **Monsters**.

Drag As 'in drag' or a 'drag queen'—male dressed as a female.

Dragon Hidden underground; suppressed emotions; the mystical and powerful part of yourself; a tradition lost; oriental, a magical protection; can be coveting something material; angry words, as in 'fire-breathing dragon'.

Drain A low point in life; eliminating old patterns; loss. What is going down the drain? See also **Sink**.

Drawing Creativity; expressing yourself; 'drawing' to a close; 'drawing on' or tapping resources.

Dress Dress, as in what girls wear; to dress, or put on clothes; 'dress a salad', or coat in dressing; new dress, new image. See also **Clothes**.

Drinking To drink in something; we often speak of drinking in love or a spiritual blessing as in Holy Communion.

Driver Someone else is controlling your life and your personal direction; or the 'lap of luxury'.

Drop 'Drop your bundle' or giving up, dropping or lowering your defenses; investigating the subconscious; dropped in a relationship, or by a friend. See also **Falling**.

Drowning Drowning in emotions; 'drowning in a sea of love', unconscious death urge; overwhelmed with problems; possessive or smothering love.

Drugs Escape from reality; changed perspective; altered consciousness; suppression and avoidance; healing the sick; natural and chemical healing substance; can be wisdom and communication in the context of tribal ritual.

Drunkenness A desire to escape from reality; to suppress fear.

Dual Two; double, as in 'dual ownership'

Duck Avoid or 'duck' some problem; comfortable—'took to it like a duck to water', 'duck dive'; a 'sitting duck'.

Duel Conflict; battle with someone; a contest; 'duel to the death'.

Dumb Being struck dumb happens frequently in nightmares. See also **Mute**.

Dungeon Subterranean cell; trapped; relates to the pits of your subconscious.

Dusk Shade darker than twilight; near the end of a project.

Dust 'Dust to dust, ashes to ashes', to dust, clear away dust; dust off. See also **Ashes, Dirt**.

Dwarf Feeling 'dwarfed' by someone more powerful, made to look small; hindered growth.

Dynamite Set up for an explosion; 'it's dynamite', a great idea. See also **Bomb, Explosion**.

Ee... Express your every fear, hurt and anger on your dream excursions. They are essential adventures of self-expression drawing on your natural resourcefulness, changing the frequency of your energy, freeing your passion.

Eagle Powerful bird of prey; soaring to great heights in life; a higher perspective; 'eagle-eyed'—sharp vision. See also **Birds**.

Ear Anything to do with hearing; your auditory gift, clairaudience (ability to hear spirit voices) or clear hearing; who do or don't you want to hear, what are you sick of hearing about yourself or what are you longing to hear?

Earth Symbol of the feminine, the 'mother' earth; life force; foundations.

Earthquake Shake-up; emotional or physical upheaval.

East The left brain—rational, logical, linear analysis and sequential time.

Eating Consuming; as sustenance for the body, mind and soul.

Eel 'Slippery as an eel', oriental symbol of prosperity or birth.

Egg New life; new idea. See also **Birth**.

Eight Authority; self-confidence; balance of spiritual and material; power; balancing of regenerative energy; eight is 'as above, so below'.

Electrician The part of you, or someone else, who helps to bring you conscious awareness, 'put the lights on'; as spirit fire—the electrical flash of inspiration that manifests as goose bumps, or goose flesh, and is often a message from your Higher Self; may refer to an electrician you know in waking life.

Elephant Power; strength; rarity; majesty; loyalty; memory; protection.

Elevator See **Lift**.

Eleven A master number; revelation; intuition; psychic or spiritual.

Emeralds Associated with Venus Roman goddess of love and beauty, for whom the planet Venus (the morning and evening star) was named; historically has symbolised 'protection from above'.

Emotions Emotions in dreams reflect back to you what you are feeling inside; use them as a guide to discerning the essence of your conscious and unconscious issues; they are more important than the setting, characters, symbols and the action in your dreams.

Empty Nothing is left; reached the end-point, the 'bottom of the barrel'; no more to give; feeling a void within, or hopeless.

Enemy The enemy within you, or the enemy outside you; 'public enemy'. Are you the victim or the victor? See also **Battle**.

Engineer Authority figure, Higher Self, God; Who is the engineer of your life?

Entry To enter a new phase of life; gain entry to a part of yourself.

Envelope Enveloped; enclosed; 'signed, sealed and delivered'.

Eruption Situations or emotions building up to exploding point; an eruption of anger; no regard for influence on other people.

Escalator See **Lift**.

Evening Not clear about something; 'in the dark'; the time just before, as Christmas Eve.

Exam Being tested; what did you learn from the situation you're in? As a life-test; a fear of failure; if faced with an exam in waking life, you may be living out various fears in your dream time.

Execution To carry out a plan, as to 'execute' something in your life, or make it happen; often it's the end or completion of something; can also relate to a past life-time.

Executioner Unconscious feelings of guilt; losing control and not thinking clearly, as in 'I lost my head'.

Exile Outcast; banished; sent away.

Exit The way out of a building, of a difficult situation, of a commitment, as in 'exit clause'.

Expensive Rich; luxurious; good quality; costly in terms of personal sacrifice.

Explosion Situation or emotions building up to exploding point; an explosion of energy or creativity. See also **Bomb, Dynamite**.

Eye The way we see things; the gift of vision or clairvoyance, clear seeing; can be the eye of God; 'I' or ego self.

Eyebrows Raising a question; third eye chakra, the site of psychic awareness, outflow and intuition is between the eyebrows.

Ff... Forgive yourself for failures; this is your responsibility. Only then can your dream teacher care for, protect and lead you to a stronger spiritual and mental consciousness. First serve yourself, then others.

Face Facing your problem; how the world sees you, hence 'open face' (honest) or 'two-faced' (one who says one thing to one person, something different to another); oriental, to 'lose face', 'loss of face', is shameful or a loss of self-esteem.

Factory Something that needs to be worked on; or cooperative industry and production; can, literally, be where you work.

Faeces Accumulated waste in your life; things you want to release or let go of. See also **Defecate, Diarrhoea**.

Fairy Elemental spirit; magical being with wings said to live in flowers; your Higher Self; protectress; femininity; goodness; a male homosexual.

Fall To make a mistake, as in 'falling down'; to give in or 'fall down on the job', falling in someone's esteem; an unavoidable journey into the depths of the subconscious.

Falling Falling from grace or favour; out of the race; humility; defeat; fear of falling is a natural fear and common in children's dreams; in adults' dreams it indicates a fear of being out of control; may indicate astral travelling. See also **Drop**.

Family May literally represent your family; family traditions; family ties. The death of your family in a dream can help to remind you of your true feelings of love, regardless of the current issues you may have with the members of your family in your waking life.

Famous person May embody certain qualities which apply to you or someone around you. Find the qualities you attribute to this person, and see how they apply in the context of the dream—even famous people as archetypes, such as Madonna.

Farm Your rural or natural self; a source of food; the provider in you; unpretentious, as in 'down on the farm', earthy; country life; cultivating or farming.

Fast Speeding towards your goals; do something quickly, be a 'fast' woman; abstain from eating, as on religious fast days, for health reasons, or as a spiritual practice.

Fat Protecting the self; wealth; a health warning; contentment and plenty.

Father Literally, your father or father-figure; your own 'paternal' nature.

FBI Who or what do you need to investigate in your life?

Feather Lightweight; spiritual symbol; ritual; uplifting ideas; a message; something you're pleased with, as in 'a feather in your cap'.

Feet How you move through life, your emotional foundations.

Female Bearing offspring; anima; goddess; compassion; See also **Feminine**.

Feminine Intuition; receptivity; gentleness; birth; caring; trust; nurturing; associated with right-brain functions.

Fence Barrier or protection; 'keep out'; or to keep in; trapped or fenced in.

Ferry Emotional voyage; observe your emotions; ferry across; aided in life.

Fertiliser Nourishment; what is needed for abundant growth in life.

Field Freedom; expansive wandering lost or aimless; can be indecision.

Fight Conflict; competition; duel; who or what are you fighting, perhaps it's yourself?

Film Skin, coating, layer, veil or haze; to film: see **Movie**.

Fingers Creativity; manipulation; touching; healing; nurturing.
  Thumb Will-power; self-control; to be 'under the thumb', squashed.
  Index Pointing finger, as direction, accusation, spiritual purpose.
  Middle Balance, achievement and leadership.
  Ring Commitment, creativity in relationships; spiritual purpose.
  Little Independence and individuality; family and groups.

Fire Warmth; passion; destruction; rage; 'fired up', enthusiastic;

'spirit fire' of deliverance; the element fire as a spiritual purification.

Fireman Authority figure; rescuer; will he put out your fire?

Fish Emotional or spiritual issues; a shoal or school of fish, moving in unison with others; hetrosexuality; early symbol of Christianity; suspicious, as in 'smells a bit fishy'.

Fist Strength; determination; clenched fist a sign of anger, rebellion or rage.

Five The number of power, change, balance and freedom; can also be the number of self-indulgence and addiction.

Flag Patriotism, nationality; loyalty to; as signals or a warning; a flag to rally the troops.

Flame Illuminating something; passion; cleansing; spiritually purifying; an old boyfriend or girlfriend, as in 'an old flame'.

Flies An irritation; they feed on 'rubbish' or carrion; carry dirt and disease.

Float Emotionally buoyant; happiness; peace; safe, as floating in the womb; moving with the flow of life; can indicate that you are astral-travelling.

Flood Floods of emotion, especially tears or sadness; 'flooded with feelings; joy; awe.

Floor Foundation; support; bottom-line; floor-plan, map of building, even of the self; 'take the floor'—public speaking.

Flowers Blossoming relationship; love; growing potential; achievements; love and romance; new experiences; literally, the genitals of plant.

Flying Moving to greater heights in your life; 'flying free', 'flights of fantasy', expanded perspective or astral travel in your dream time. See also **Aeroplane**.

Fog Emotional confusion; lacking clarity in thought or vision; hazy; poor visibility.

Food Sustenance; nurturing; a warning about your health or dietary advice.

Foot 'Foot the bill' or pay a debt. See also **Feet**.

Forest Unknown territory; natural self; instincts; down-to-earth.

Foreign Any unknown person or thing; as in 'foreign object', odd or unusual; insecurity, as in feeling 'foreign'.

Fort fortress Barrier; protection; anticipating a conflict, to fortify or arm.

Foundation Support; the 'foundation' of a problem, the basis of your current issue.

Fountain Youth, as in 'the fountain of youth'; spiritual rejuvenation; light-heartedness; joy; love; an overflowing of the emotions.

Four Practical discipline, initiation, serious work, wholeness, all types of foundations, including personal integrity. Four is the number of form; self-mastery, building and constructing; industry, technology and organisation.

Fox Cunning; sexy, as in 'a foxy lady'; witty; sly, as in 'sly as a fox'.

Fragile Something easily lost or broken; be careful.

Fridge See **Refrigerator**.

Friend May be a friend in your waking life, or someone who wants to help you; also may reflect other aspects of yourself, often possessing similar qualities to the particular friend in your dream.

Frightened Feeling fearful in your dreams is pointing you to an area of fear in your waking life. Confront what is frightening you in your dream. Invent a dream weapon to protect you.

Frigid Restrained sexuality; barriers; 'cold' or unwelcome reception.

Frog Bounding through life; taking a leap in the right direction.

Front Conscious awareness; presentation to the world; 'it's a front'—fake; to 'front up' to someone—to confront them, give them cheek or call them on an issue; be 'upfront'—to tell the truth.

Front seat Directing own life; in control; in charge.

Front yard Conscious mind and thoughts; how you present yourself to the world.

Frozen 'Frozen out'—forced to leave; 'frozen' assets—unavailable funds. See also **Cold**.

'Frozen' See **Cannot move, Paralysed**.

Fruit Health and vitality; nourishment; 'a fruit'—a male homosexual; crazy, as in 'nutty as a fruitcake'.

Fuel Anything that is converted to energy.

Funeral Death; some unhealthy or rigid part of yourself has died; burying old ideas and habits; or, literally, a funeral you may hear of or attend. See also **Death, Coffin, Corpse.**

Fur Animal instincts; hair; wealth, warmth and protection.

Furniture The accessories in your life; what you furnish, provide in life.

Gg... *Give yourself the time to reflect on what, in the detached state of sleep, you see with clarity. Your dormant thoughts and true feelings will all be exposed for your greater understanding; here are the keys that take you through the gate.*

Gaia The earth goddess or the soul of awareness of the earth that evolves along with earth's inhabitants.

Galah A fool, as in 'stupid galah'; literally, your pet. See also **Birds**.

Galaxy Infinite possibilities or potential.

Gamble Taking a gamble in life; taking or running a risk.

Game Treat it lightly; you don't take it seriously enough; have more fun.

Gaol See **Prison**.

Garage A 'pit-stop', a pause in life; where have you parked yourself in life?

Garbage Often a symbol for your 'emotional garbage'. See also **Rubbish**.

Garden How you present yourself to the world; your natural self. Front garden: in full view, conscious mind. Back garden: what is hidden, unconscious mind.

Garnets Offer protection from injury; improve circulation and lift energy.

Gas Energy.

Gate The way you come in and the way you go out; protection; are you locked away inside yourself?

Gay Exploring fears and fantasies, for both men and women, embracing and learning to love the inner female or male aspect of yourself.

Genitals Issues around sex and sexuality; sexual power; procreation. See also **Balls, Penis, Scrotum, Vagina, Womb**.

Ghost A visitor from your past; past actions catching up with you; someone whose actions you can clearly see through; a vague memory; ghostly, a shade or a shadow; literally, a ghost or soul without a physical body; can be a ghost attached to a particular environment, as in 'haunted house'.

Giant A large threatening person or thing; may also be a childhood memory.

Gift Giving something or a part of the self away; acknowledgment being received from or given to someone else; or a gift of gratitude.

Girl The girl inside you; girlish behaviour; may, literally, be a girl you know; if male, your anima.

Girlfriend May, literally, be your girlfriend; sign of friendship and love; feeling close to the female part of yourself.

Glass Clear view; if broken, could indicate danger or broken dreams; if dirty, unclear view of future; barrier to intimacy ('into-me-see'). See also **Cup**.

Glasses A dim view; can't see clearly; something needs magnifying or re-focusing.

Glove Protection; worn as part of a uniform.

Glue Solution to a problem; trying to keep things 'glued' together.

Goat Acting the goat—making a fool of yourself; stubborn.

Goblin Fear and uncertainty, especially in children's dreams. See also **Monster**.

God The Great Spirit; Higher Self; however you see a particular spiritual authority figure or figures as gods.

Goddess The female face, aspect, nature, and/or essence of God.

Gold A symbol of wealth; also represents masculine energy; energy of the sun; conscious energy that is by nature 'true'; spiritual protection; richness; aspiration; purity; quality; goodness, as in 'as good as gold'.

Goldfish Serene; calm; peaceful. See also **Fish, Pet**.

Gold (rose) Because of copper content, is a good electrical conductor; believed to assist in 'channelling' the highest or holy spirits.

Gorge Pitfall; depths of the subconscious; feed greedily; gluttonous.

Gorilla A threatening power.

Gossip May refer literally to gossip in your own life; prying;

opinionated; 'busybody', 'sticking your nose' into other people's business.

Grail As in holy grail; quest or search for Higher Self or truth.

Grandparents May, literally, be your grandparents; ancestor; age; a spirit guardian.

Grass Growth; cultivation; constancy; natural self; 'grass', as in marijuana—, suppresses sadness, escaping reality.

Grave Being responsible for your actions, as in 'digging your own grave'; feeling as though there's no way out of your current situation; a serious or 'grave' situation; 'beyond the grave'—journeying into the unknown; the pit of your subconscious mind.

Grease Anoint; 'grease the palm'—a bribe; a grease and oil change; greasy food. See also **Oil**.

Green Growth; constancy; expansion of new horizons, harmony and love; 'green with envy'; 'green'—inexperienced or immature.

Greenhouse Cultivated growth; greenhouse effect or global warming.

Grey Halfway between black and white; 'grey and gloomy'.

Groper Someone sexually harassing; uncertain, as in 'groping' for ideas, 'groping in the dark', 'groping' for life's answers.

Ground Grounded; earthed; protection; foundation; a solid base; 'ground to a pulp', ground as in minced meat.

Growth Personal growth and understanding; flourishing; expansion; any type of constant, gradual change.

Guard May be a side of yourself or someone else who takes on the role of guarding and protecting you; alertness, or being 'on guard'.

Guardian Higher Self; guardian angel; a physical or spiritual protector, Holy Spirit.

Guide Higher Self; someone who has acted as a guide or teacher in your life; guiding yourself.

Guillotine Losing your head; can be past-life memory.

Gun Freudian phallic symbol. See also **Weapon**.

Guru Venerable one; religious teacher; way-shower. See also **Prophet, Guide, Guardian**.

Gutter Low life or 'in the gutter'.

Gypsy Passion; restless; mysterious; psychic powers.

Hh... Harness that which creates success for you. Hold tight as you ride the night mare and steer her to the place above, where there is no fear, and where everything that brings you happiness is waiting.

Hair Thoughts, thinking; attitudes, beliefs; personal power; virility; spiritual beauty; white hair a sign of wisdom. See also **Bald**.

Hall, hallway Narrow range of options; on a 'long haul'. See also **Alley**.

Hammer Precision; accuracy; constructing your own life; persisting and 'hammering' in an idea.

Handcuff Helplessness; your 'hands are tied'; who or what are you bound to?

Hands Creativity; manipulation; touching; healing; nurturing.

Hanging Suspended; 'hang on'—wait; 'hang up', as clothes; 'hang-up', as issue or problem; can be death by hanging, possibly a past-life recollection.

Harassment Persisting; unwanted attention. Do you see yourself as a victim?

Harbour Especially emotions; hide, shelter, protect or 'harbour' someone.

Hardware See **Tools**.

Hare See **Rabbit**.

Harpoon Tool for attack, especially on whales; defence. See also **Weapon**.

Hat Image presented to the world; part of a uniform or position; may have past-life connections; making affiliations known, who do you support?

Haunted house Your past creeping into your present. See also **Ghost**.

Haven See **Sanctuary**.

Haze Unable to see something clearly. See also **Fog**.

Head Intellectual concerns; mental stress; thoughts, concepts and beliefs. See also **Right-brain, Left-brain**.

Headaches Withheld emotions; anger; sexual frustration or fear.

Headlights Searching for direction; a goal in view.

Heart Chakra or centre of love, receiving love or support; heartbreak—overwhelming grief or defeat; heart shape—a gift of love; imminent love affair.

Heart attack Inability to receive love; feeling unloved or unlovable; fear of intimacy; lover's attack; in some cases, a prophetic dream of physical heart attack.

Heat Experiencing trouble; urgency, as in 'the heat is on'; anger, as in 'heated discussions'.

Heaven Feeling wonderful; a wonderful place; reaping the rewards of your virtuous efforts.

Heel Achilles heel—hidden weakness; 'heel' as in creep, unpleasant social misfit; 'heel' as in 'come to heel'—command given to working dogs; repressed, as in 'under the heel'.

Helicopter Viewing life from a higher perspective; manoeuvring well through life.

Hell Feeling horrible; a terrible, hopeless place; suppressed guilt; 'hell to pay'—paying for your sins; living 'a hell on earth'; 'giving someone hell' or a bad time; 'come hell and high water—I will do it!'; a good or bad time, as in 'a hell of a time'.

Hermit Isolation; aloneness; solitude; may be a need to meditate, go within.

Hill Rising to greater heights in your life; an obstacle to overcome.

Hit Successful attempt, as in 'direct hit'; core; 'hit it off' or agree. See also **Fight**.

Hole A low point in your life; a pitfall to be aware of; into the unconscious and subconscious mind. See also **Ditch**.

Holiday Take a break; relaxation; pleasure; adventure; escape; change; renewal of personal energy.

Home Symbol of the self. See also **House**.

Homosexuality See **Gay, Lesbian**.

Honey Spiritual food of love; 'he/she's a honey'—sweet person.

Hook A lure to catch something; an often unwanted attachment as a 'drama hook', an emotional leverage.

Horizon Looking to the distant future; expansive awareness.

Horn 'Blowing your own horn'—self-praise; wake up; phallic symbol, as in 'horny'.

Horse Carrier; messenger; sexual libido, passion; mode of transport for past generations; a dream horse—either the nightmare or (winged) Pegasus.

Hose Depending on dream context, a phallic symbol; fun; time to 'cool off'; to 'hose down'.

Hospital Illness; surgery; confinement; the healing part of yourself; a need for attention and nurturing or healing consciousness for treating a problem.

Hostel The adventurous part of yourself; community involvement.

Hot 'Hot news'—the latest information; under pressure, as in 'the heat is on'; embarrassment; anger, rage and passion.

Hotel A symbol of yourself; a temporary state of living; living it up; travelling to new areas in your life; sharing yourself with many other people.

Hot water In deep trouble.

House A symbol of your self; the whole self—physical, emotional, mental and spiritual aspects. See also individual rooms, **Attic**, **Basement**, etc.

Hovel Poverty; in state of disrepair; spiritually destitute, or poor in spirit.

Hunch Conceive an idea; suspects something; a premonition of something.

Hungry Needing nourishment and nurturing; unsatisfied; hungry for knowledge, love, purpose and awareness.

Hunted Under attack; being desired; feeling threatened by someone.

Hunting Searching for something or someone in your life; attacking others.

Hurricane A storm with violent winds; windswept—inner confusion needs release.

Husband May, literally, be your husband; could also be the 'husband-like' aspect of yourself. Check what qualities you attribute to a 'husband', and see how these apply to yourself.

Ii... *Improvements often come indirectly. Our dreams though seemingly muddled are intense impressions that drive us to reflect inwardly on what ideals we can evolve within ourselves.*

Ice Emotional coldness, frigidity; something is frozen in your life; slippery; dangerous, as in 'on thin ice'; 'breaking the ice'—introduction to friendship.

Ice cream Treats; indulgence; nurturing, sharing, friendship, especially in the dreams of children.

Idol Worship false gods; materialism; idolise or put up on a pedestal.

Illness Unhealthy conditions, a symbol of unease; a need to resolve issues or inner problems may indicate the metaphysical cause of illness or disease.

Immobile See **Cannot move.**

Impotence Lacking power; can't keep it up; feeling ineffectual in any area of life; you may be playing out a fear of actual impotence in your dream time.

Incest Sexual abuse from a family member. Often occurs in dreams when victims of abuse are emotionally mature enough to confront their issue and heal the inner child. A warning: be sure you have evidence of sexual abuse in your childhood, such as dysfunctional personal relationships, emotional problems, low self-esteem. Dreams of incest can also relate to any 'suppressed incest pattern', Freud's Electra and Oedipus complex, where you may dream a secret or subconscious fantasy; may also be symbolic of blending yourself with the 'parent' inside of you; making peace and love with a parent. Seek professional help or join a group for victims of sexual abuse.

Infant Inner child; childish or infantile part of self; childlike innocence and wonder.

Infection Depression; something is deeply affecting you; infected by other's values or unease in a dream. If acted on in time can avoid the creation of this disease in your waking life. The purpose of a prophetic dream is to avert disaster, not confirm it.

Inheritance Gains in life; genetic memory; inherited genes; beliefs and concepts.

Initiation Introduction; the beginning; tests and rituals; acceptance of a path; a challenge. See also **Ceremony**.

Injection Penetration; an injection of ideas; being influenced, as on drugs; healing. See also **Darts, Needle**.

Injury A part of the self or of someone else who has been wounded. Gain clues from the function of the body part that has been wounded. Left or right side of body.

Insect Being 'bugged' (annoyed) psychic attack; parasites; malice, negative vibrations. See also **Ant, Bee**.

Instruction Lesson; learning; being shown or being told what to do and how to do it.

Interview If facing an interview in your waking life, you may be playing out your fears in your dream time; answering for your actions, as in a police interview; putting your best side forward.

Intruder Feeling invaded or intruded upon by someone or something. Is it a welcome intruder, the spunk you have the hots for or an unwelcome intruder you need to confront by setting clear boundaries in the situation?

Invasion Invasion of one's space, privacy or thoughts; intergalactic invasion or communication. See also **Alien**.

Invention A creation; a symbol of your true creative power.

Invisible Something in your life that can't be seen; hidden from view.

Iron Solve a problem, as in 'iron things out'; persisting, as in 'pressing' the point; a 'pressing situation'.

Island Isolation; secluded; an uninhibited paradise.

Itchy An irritation; who or what is most irritating to you?; feeling attacked by something or someone; mental or psychic attack.

Jj... Journey through your dreamscapes with abandon. Fear not; trust that your guide is good-natured, wise and ethical. Know that your very happiness is where the tour will end.

Jade Recognised for its healing properties; the Chinese believe jade imbues the wearer with charity, courage, wisdom, modesty, justice; Maoris believe jade offers long life and fertility.

Jail See **Prison**.

Jar See **Bottle**.

Jaw Seat of pent-up anger, rage and resentment; a desire for revenge.

Jaywalk Breaking rules; taking your life into your hands; authority issues; travelling against the flow of convention; being individual.

Jealousy Feeling rejected, left out, insecure.

Jetty A place to get a detached view of your emotional state.

Jewel Something precious.

Jewellery Something precious; life's accessories; what you value in life; may signify a symbol of personal empowerment given to you by your Higher Self in a dream—if you recall the stone, metal or shape, look for further meaning by cross-referencing with other symbols. See also **Necklace**, **Ring**.

Job Work; any issues around your job.

Journal Be aware of what's happening to you; take note!

Journey Your life's journey. Can actually be prophetic if planning a holiday. The trick is to work out if it is your past, present or future journey.

Judge The part of yourself or someone else which judges you, judges your actions and the actions of others around you; weighs up both sides of an issue.

Jump 'Jump for joy' or 'jump in fright'. See also **Leap**.

Jungle Exploring the unfamiliar aspects of yourself; adventure; wilderness.

Jury Explaining your actions; being called to account for your actions; guilty feelings; if a jury member, you are being called on to judge someone else's actions; unanimous decisions; responsibility.

Kk... Kindergarten fears sit quietly in the backyards of our adulthood. The Dream Teacher leads us back to them forcefully. Confronting and dealing with those fears brings to our inner child a new perspective of gaiety, cheer and excitement.

Kangaroo Moving through life in leaps and bounds.

Key Solution to a problem or issue; opens new doors.

Keyhole Where is the key?

Kill Killing off some negative part of yourself; or acting out your suppressed aggression.

King King of your world; authority figure; pompous attitudes; ruler. See also **Chief**.

Kiss A bonding; an expression of love or lust; the 'kiss of death'—betrayal.

Kitchen Issues around nourishing and nurturing; love, friendship, warmth. See also **Dining Room**.

Kitten Catty; your sexual instincts; sensual; 'playful as a kitten'; 'sex kitten'. See also **Cat**.

Knee Inflexibility; pride and stubbornness; unbending ideas or fear of change.

Knife Attack; cutting through problems. See also **Cut, Weapon**.

Knight Warrior; protector; brave; your hero, as in 'knight in shining armour'.

Knitting To mend a rift or break, as in bones; bringing things together; creative, as a form of weaving.

Knock An opportunity or higher awareness attempting to get your attention.

Knot Point of confusion or difficulty; untie a knot; 'tie the knot'—unite, wed.

Koala Seeing things from a higher perspective; slow-minded; cute, cuddly.

Ll... Love each gentle, colourful, expressive, romantic moment of your twilight zone. The stars that sprinkle dust and the moon that soothes the dark crevices are as real as all else that uplifts you.

Label Being labelled a particular 'type of person'; judging; identification.

Laboratory The experimental part of yourself; to find answers, use the mind.

Ladder Climbing to a higher perspective step by step; spiritual growth, ascension; climbing the 'ladder of success'.

Lake Water—a symbol of the emotions; if smooth, placid; if rough, turmoil; can symbolise contained emotions or spiritual wisdom; mystical knowledge. See also **Water**.

Lamb Sacrifice; Lamb of God; gentleness, vulnerability; spring lambs.

Lame Weak, as in 'lame excuse'; crippled; misunderstood, mental or psychological hurt; crippling pain.

Lamp Illumination and understanding; a spiritual light; way-showing.

Landlord, landlady Authority figures; wealth or influence.

Laser Intense light beam; any concentration of energy; piercing focus.

Late 'Too late'—a missed opportunity; unconscious avoidance of something or someone.

Laundry Issues around cleansing away unwanted issues or patterns.

Law Universal law; Karmic laws; laws of life; laws of abundance.

Lawn Your natural self; self-growth; cultivating a skill; if green, fulfilling; if brown, barren or unproductive.

Lawnmower Shaping your skills; clipping your growth;.

Lawyer See **Solicitor**.

Leader Your leadership qualities; any guide; chief; the first in a field.

Leap Moving ahead quickly; 'leap into the unknown'; ' a leap of faith'.

Leaves Symbol of growth; accomplishment; achievements; falling in autumn; all completions, endings and renewals.

Lecturer Someone who can teach you something; getting a lecture if in difficulty or trouble; your Higher Self; the teacher within you; may, literally, be a lecturer in your dream time; also, any lecturer you know in waking life.

Leech Someone draining you, physically or mentally; spiritually or emotionally sucked dry.

Left Injuries; choices; hit from the left; any dream where you are aware it's the left side relates to the feminine or intuitive side (connected to the right-brain).

Left-brain Connected to the right side of the body and the masculine focus, its functions are: analytical; logical; rational; differential; sequential; serial time; explicit; active; the left-brain focus is through relationships and inferred intuition.

Legs How you move through life; the focus of your personal direction.

Leopard Cunning; dangerous; wild feminine qualities; predatory instinct; sensuality; wild; changing alliances, as in 'leopard changing its spots'.

Lesbian Exploring female homosexual fears and fantasies; for both men and women, embracing or learning to love inner female or male aspect of yourself.

Letter Corresponding with self; message; from friends and loved ones.

Library The part of yourself dedicated to study and learning through books; being 'led' to information you need; knowledge at hand.

Lice Irritation; feeling attacked; a manifestation of your own anger; someone or something not coming up to expectations, as in 'lousy'.

Licence Permission; authority; a permit of some kind.

Lid To confine a problem, as 'put a lid on it'; hold something in.

Lift Way to higher consciousness; up to enlightenment or down into your subconscious.

Light Illumination; enlightenment; awareness; come out of the dark. Inner spiritual light; electro-magnetic light; bio-electrical aura.

Lighthouse Shedding light and awareness on something.

Lightning A bolt of awareness; high energy; pure spirit fire; electricity.

Lilac Rebirth, death of the old, birth of the new, a spiritual or personal transformation.

Lily A symbol of purity and resurrection.

Lingerie Sex life; sensuality; symbol of femininity.

Lion Pride; ego; power; strength; courage, as in 'lion heart'; feline qualities;

Lips Self-expression; sensuality.

Load A burden; loading up something, or someone.

Loan Borrowing something from others; lending to others.

Lobster Lives in the ocean depths, a symbol of the deep unconscious mind; a symbol of Scorpio; sometimes a symbol of armour or protection.

Lock 'Locked away'—inaccessible; locked-in emotions; locked out of—first find the key.

Lost Lacking direction; you've lost your way in life; you've lost something or someone.

Loungeroom Issues around relaxation; entertaining and communication or sharing.

Love You will dream your greatest fears and fantasies as you learn to love yourself and others unconditionally.

Luggage Can mean actual travel; desired travel; perhaps emotional or psychological baggage. See also **Briefcase**.

Mm... *Marvel at yourself the master-builder, and the magical way you adapt everything that comes your way. You have learned well from your Dream Teacher, who has little more than the stray symbols from your memory to construct your dreams for a better reality.*

Machine Doing something automatically; constant repetition; or unfeeling.

Magazine Messages; serials; watch for details; information; hot gossip.

Magic Something mysterious; the unknown; the inexplicable; the magic of life.

Magician That part of yourself or someone else who brings magic and mystery into your life; someone you don't trust, whose hand moves faster than the eye.

Magnet Any attraction that is irresistable.

Magus Member of an ancient Persian priestly caste; Magi or sorcerers, as 'the three wise men' present at the birth of Christ, often appear as spirit guides in dreams.

Maid See **Servant**.

Make-up Your personality; how you present yourself to the world; a mask; 'war-paint';

Male If female, may be animus. See also **Man, Masculine** and **Left-brain**.

Man Masculine qualities within you; literally, a man you know in waking life. See also **Masculine** and **Left-brain**.

Mandala Circular meditation symbol or painting used as a focus of religious worship. See also **Circle**.

Maniac Senseless; deranged, unacceptable thoughts or feelings; madness.

Mansion Wealth; a rich and expansive part of yourself; the many parts of you.

Map Seeking or finding spiritual or personal direction.

Marble Ancient memories; can be immortal beauty; gracious living.

Marijuana Suppresses sadness; an escape from reality; smoked in reefers, joints, pipes or bongs. See also **Drugs, Grass**.

Marriage A blending of opposites, as opposite sexes; unity; initiation; trust; bond between a man and a woman; vows and promises ; if you are already married or are about to be married, you will probably live out in your dream time all your fears and fantasies associated with commitment.

Martial arts Self-defence; attack; danger.

Martyr Is your sacrifice worth it? Is your cause worth dying for?

Masculine Creative aggression; power; logic; decisiveness; strength; leadership. See also **Male, Man**.

Mask Concealed; hidden; not showing your true self, as in 'hiding behind a mask'. See also **Make-up**.

Massage Relaxation; healing; for self or others; a gift of healing.

Masturbation Sexual awakening, unconscious fear of intimacy; unresolved trauma or sexual issues; living out fears and fantasies in your dream time.

Matron See **Nurse**.

Mauve See Lilac.

Maze A-maze-ment; puzzlement; web of intrigue; searching for a solution; the maze of life.

Meadow Green—growth; renewal, balance, at one with nature; brown—barren. See also **Field**.

Meat Sharing a feast; good company; rotten meat—danger or a warning.

Medicine Problem being treated; take the consequences of your actions, as in 'take your medicine' or 'a taste of your own medicine'.

Meeting Bringing together ideas; consolidation; resolution; joining and unity.

Menstruation Letting go of the old; a cyclic cleansing; issues around femininity; initiation into womanhood.

Mermaid, merman An aspect of your emotional, right-brain, intuitive self; often your sexual self.

Merry-go-round Following the same old path; round in circles, indecision; joy; fun; childhood freedom.

Messenger Most frequently it's your Higher Self, or else the postman or a more mundane message you are expecting in your waking life.

Microphone A need to project yourself; your truth; being heard.

Microscope Something hard to see or unseen, finding a hidden truth or the answer within.

Middle path Conservatism; a balance in all things.

Milk Sustenance; nurturing; nourishment, as 'milk of human kindness'.

Minister Authority figure. See also **Priest**.

Mirror Face yourself; time for reflection; reflecting the truth; can represent the Hindu philosophy of Maya or illusion, the unreal or individual reflection of reality; can be a past life; what do you see in your reflections?

Miscarriage Not going ahead with your plans or with a project; if pregnant, may represent a fear being played out in dream time.

Miser Mean person; withholding love or support from others.

Missing A train, boat, bus, plane etc.—life is passing you by; in the right place at the wrong time; you have missed an opportunity. See also **Late**.

Model The ideal, as in 'model parent'; concept; archetype.

Monastery The deeply religious side of yourself; celibacy; issues around sex and sexuality; repenting for 'sins'; retreat from the world; brotherhood or sisterhood. Black, brown or grey garments.

Money Payment; energy exchange; achievements; issues around money, may also be issues around love or personal values; a desire for wealth. See also **Coins, Cost**.

Monk Vows and holy orders; religious beliefs; inner church (temple of the soul or physical body) and outer church (the church you attend in your waking life). See also **Monastery**.

Monkey The trickster; instinctive energy; naughty; joking around, making a 'monkey' of yourself; protective; group energy—'monkey see monkey do'; 'monkey on the back', as for an addict. See also **Monastery**.

Monster The symbol of your unconscious fears, especially in children's dreams; an unacknowledged part of yourself that you are still afraid of seeing or expressing; insecurity; a victim; fear of attack from outside yourself; may symbolise someone you consider to be awful, or a 'monster'. See also **Goblin**, **Devil**.

Monument Dedication or honour; up on a pedestal; historical reminder.

Moon Feminine energy; intuition; tides and cycles of life; 'once in a blue moon',—rarely; wildness and instinctual emotions; sorrow, depression, madness. (lunatics are influenced by the full moon); sexuality; secret; mystery.

Morning Awakening; dawn of an idea; brightness of future; new perspective.

Mosquito A persistent irritation; a manifestation of your own anger.

Motel Roadside hotel; place to stay; travel haven; sleazy one-night stand.

Moth Changes in life; moving without knowledge of true destiny, 'like a moth to a flame'. See also **Butterfly**.

Mother Literally, your mother; authority figure; a mother-figure; unconditional love and support; your own 'maternal' nature.

Motorbike Speeding through life, enjoying the wind in your hair; freedom; a symbol of rebelliousness.

Mountain Spiritual goal; moving to a greater awareness in life; a large obstacle.

Mouse Someone with an innocuous or weak personality, as in 'mousy'; infested with vermin; 'a pest'; some problem is 'gnawing away' at you.

Mouth Any form of nourishment; communication; expression.

Movie The script or movie of your life; collective consciousness; mass mind. See also **Play**.

Movie star The person symbolises an aspect of yourself in the dream scenario.

Mud Lack of clarity, as in 'as clear as mud'; feeling stuck or thwarted.

Muddy Unclear issues or choices; confusion; emotional turmoil;

can be a barrier or veil between the seen and the unseen; the physical and the spiritual planes.

Mule See **Donkey**.

Murderer Manifestation of your fear of survival—who or what stalks you?; can be killing off a part of yourself; your suppressed murderous or evil intentions; an unconscious desire to attack, or feeling under attack, a manifestation of your unconscious rage and murderous feelings; safer for everyone if you express this in your dreams rather than in your waking life.

Museum An understanding of the past.

Music The rhythm of life; creative, emotional expression; 'to face the music' or the consequences of your actions; being 'in tune', or 'in harmony' with someone.

Musical Instruments Generally relate to personal musical preferences, depending on the instrument in your dream. Drums, percussion—primordial; harp—angelic.

Mute Ineffectual communication; lack of self-expression; 'mute with fear'—what are you afraid to say? See also **Dumb**.

Nn... *Nightingales bring new knowledge to the seeker, in flights of fancy and restless adventures. Their wings flap impatiently on the windows of your subconscious, imploring you to join them, to listen, to soar, to explore.*

Naked 'The naked truth'—your true self; your vulnerability; facing your deepest fears of being caught in the nude; unconscious issues about your body. What do you fear others can see that you don't want them to? Do you crave total freedom?

Nappy Helplessness; needing to be looked after; a time warp dream to your childhood issues around toilet-training. See also **Defecate**.

Narrow Limited options; narrow point of view; a 'narrow escape'; 'a narrow-minded' person—it could be you.

Nausea Wanting to physically reject something; fear; what are you truly sick of feeling about yourself or others?

Navel Deep conscious or unconscious links and connections to loved ones; seat of umbilical cord; 'the silver cord' that connects the soul to the body.

Neck The past; inflexibility; back of the neck—the past can also relate to genetic or past-life memories.

Necklace A status symbol; a valuable gift of love. See also **Jewellery**.

Necktie See **Tie**.

Needle Penetration; to pester someone, as in 'to needle' someone; a childhood fear of injections; an injection; any drug-related issues. See also **Injection**.

Neighbour Neighbourly; someone you're close to, in a similar situation to you.

Neon An advertising sign; something asking you to pay attention, used as highlighting device; See also **Red-light area**.

Nest Childhood home life; 'leave the nest'; as in 'next egg'; 'nesting' instinct or desire for parenthood.

Net Any catching tool; to catch or be caught; to achieve a goal; or 'net income'.

Networking Meeting, associating with and working with other people in a similar field of interest or experience.

News Any current message; any events reported; the daily news.

Newspaper Current messages; publicity; headlines, notoriety or scandal.

Nicotine An addictive drug that suppresses anger. See also **Cigarettes**.

Nightmares Living out each of your unconscious fears and negative beliefs in your dream time.

Nine An altruistic or spiritual number, and as such it represents divine love; unconditional love; nine is also the number of completion.

Nipple See **Breast**.

North Refers to the back brain and the pineal gland.

Nose Self-recognition.

Nude See **Naked**.

Numbers See individual numbers, **One, Two, Three**, etc.

Nun Celibacy; spiritual pursuits; sisterhood; may also be a nun you know in your waking life. See also **Monk, Monastery**.

Nurse A healing influence in your life; in need of healing or nurturing, as in 'nurse back to health'.

Oo... Observe yourself as you stride onwards past your fears into the dawn of another perception. Be thankful that each night's optic (visual) lesson serves you well, so that you too may serve your purpose with an open heart.

Oak Strength; endurance; a long life; the tree sacred to the Druids.

Oar Can relate to struggle in general or your life's struggle; to propel by leverage.

Oasis Paradise; source of water; emotions; richness; relief, if it's an oasis in an emotional desert.

Obese See **Fat**.

Ocean A symbol of Spirit. More frequently, a symbol of your emotions—if calm, it's peace and contentment; if rough, it's turmoil, strife and drama; if your ocean is invigorating, it may be passion; if refreshing, it's spiritual, as in a baptism.

Octopus Trapped; inextricably held by tentacles. Can relate to a situation where you are controlled by another who hinders your direction or saps your energy; strangles creativity.

Office Usually your work life; work commitments; a duty; organisation.

Official As in 'official position'; 'official letter'; authority figure.

Oil Energy; to smooth things out, keep things running; polluting yourself; an untrustworthy, 'slimy' or 'oily' person. See also **Fuel**.

Omen An object or occurrence that is often a prophetic sign—information may be either good or evil; hence 'ominous news'.

One Represents individual will; original thoughts and ideas; inspiration; leadership; new ideas and new ventures.

Opal Believed to aid in the accessing of power from 'unknown' realms; associated with the planet Pluto. Can assist the immune system.

Operation Healing influence; something in your life needs fixing; handing over your power, as when 'under the knife'.

Oracle A prophetic divination; often a spoken prophecy.

Orange Emotional energy; impulsive responses; one of the colours of health and happiness; saffron robes can denote a spiritual guide.

Orchestra Discord or harmony; unison; joy of life. See also **Music**.

Organ music Generally, a religious influence.

Orgasm An actual physical orgasm is correcting an imbalance of sexual expression in your waking life; the height of pleasure on the physical plane.

Orgy Sexual desires; excess lust that can lead to disease; exploring sexual fantasies in your dreams.

Orphan Detachment from parents' beliefs or attitudes. See also **Abandoned**.

Ostrich Not wanting to see what's going on, as in 'burying your head in the sand' See also **Birds**.

Oven Symbol of the feminine; pregnancy, as in 'bun in the oven', gestation of a project; 'cooking up' a new idea.

Overcoat Something to 'cover up'. See also **Coat**.

Owl Symbol of wisdom; wise advice or a wise decision. See also **Birds**.

Oyster Potential for great inner beauty; not showing your true self; hidden wealth, as in 'pearl of wisdom'.

Pp... *Puzzle over every clue. Each dream is a component of a parable of truth and wisdom that aids your progression towards perfection. The perplexed will always find their true purpose in this way.*

Pack 'Pack up'; 'backpack'; 'pack it in'; where are you going? See also **Luggage**.

Package A parcel; gift; a delivery, something that is yours or belongs to you.

Pain A pain in dreams is usually alerting you to emotional pain in your waking life. Physical, emotional, mental or spiritual dis-ease or unease can be prophetic. See also **Injury, Illness**.

Paint Creative medium; to paint a picture as a work of art; to decorate; renovating your house as in 'a new coat of paint'. See also **Colours**.

Painting Creative urge; many artists paint or illustrate their dreams.

Palace Richness, royalty and potential inside you; the many rooms and true majesty of your potential self.

Pantry Symbol of the feminine; mothering; nourishment; potential hidden from view.

Paper A message; if blank, time to decide on new goals, time to start afresh as in 'turn a new page'.

Parachute Any safety factor; a precaution for a safe landing.

Parade On parade; the many roles you play in life; the many parts or facets of yourself; celebration of self; fun and aliveness.

Paralysed An inability to move ahead or take action in life; fear of situations; can't cope with problems and personal issues. See also **Cannot move**.

Parents Quite literally, your own parents or guardians; the aspects of your parents which you carry around inside yourself. See also **Family, Father, Mother**.

Park Your natural self; strolling through life; community life.

Parking Stopped; temporarily halting your progress in life; pause in activity.

Partner A actual partner; alter ego; anima or animus.

Party Celebration; interaction with others; the people there may be people you know, they may be symbolic of people you know, or they may represent the many different aspects of yourself.

Passenger Someone else is responsible for your life; you're not in control, not in the driving seat.

Passport Your permit or permission to travel ahead in life; symbol of global citizenship.

Path Your life's path. Straight and you move ahead; winding you are off-course; uphill it's a challange; down can be easy or dangerous.

Patient Those you heal; can be a way your Dream Teacher is telling you to be patient with yourself or your healing process.

Pawn 'A mere pawn', as in chess; something loaned or to be later redeemed.

Peacock 'Proud as a peacock'—pride; strutting.

Peanuts Not much of a reward.

Pearls Pearls of wisdom; the jewels of love; an organic 'stone' often ground and used in love potions in the sixteenth century.

Pen The ability to express yourself; communicate, be understood.

Pencil Get to the point; sharpen up! See also **Pen**.

Pendulum Time and change; moving back and forth in life; balance.

Penetration Sexual or attack; feeling invaded.

Penis Sexual issues; body issues; masculine power; aggression; potency; procreation. See also **Genitals, Snake**.

Perfume Sensuality; femininity; one of the odours of life.

Peridot Symbolises happiness in marriage, freedom from insecurity, both emotional and physical.

Periods Measure of time. See also **Menstruation**.

Perspiration See **Sweat**.

Pet Your animal instincts, which you have trained or 'domesticated' so they are under your control. See also individual animals.

Petrol Energy. See also **Fuel**.

Phone See **Telephone**.

Photo Memory; a particular time; a time warp dream; a memory jog; remember this?

Physician A symbol of self-healing. See also **Doctor**.

Piano In tune with someone; in harmony; fun. See also **Music**.

Picture How you see things; 'picture this', 'one picture is worth a thousand words'.

Pie Food for football games; corporate pie and your piece of it.

Pig Excess or greed as in 'pigging-out'; selfish; 'dirty pig'—filthy; 'pig-headed'; stubborn; 'pig-sty'—slovenly, messy; 'happy as a pig in poo'.

Pigeon Messenger. See also **Birds**.

Pill To take the unpleasant consequences of your actions, as in 'a bitter pill to swallow'; suppression; healing.

Pillow See **Cushion**.

Pilot Usually your Higher Self; the co-pilot who is directing your life's course.

Pine Clarity; refreshing; to 'pine away for someone'.

Pirate Someone who is draining your emotional energy. See also **Burglar**.

Piss Beer, as 'on the piss'; to tease, as in 'take the piss out of someone'. See also **Urinate**.

Pit Base emotions; subconscious mind; stuck in a 'rut'; 'it's the pits'; an abyss.

Plane As in 'a higher plane'; flying or moving through life with a higher perspective; spiritual awareness; actual air travel; many people do dream of air crashes—often this is a way in which your Dream Teacher shows you your own safety in this area. See also **Flying**.

Planets Universal awareness; astrological interpretations.

Plants Symbol of growth in your life; healing; greens, salads.

Plastic Moulded, flexible; bogus, fake or artificial.

Plates Serving others; platters of abundance; a joyous bounty or bones and scraps—whatever life is serving you.

Play The roles you play in life; games of life; past, present and future—acts one, two and three. See also **Movie**.

Plumbing 'The waterworks'—urinary functions and organs; elimination of wastes. See also **Bathroom**.

Pocket Putting a part of yourself away; concealed or hiding; top pocket may represent pride and image, as in 'sports captain', control, as in 'has him in her pocket'.

Poem, poetry Essence; the 'feel' of something; lyrical; rhyming, metered, verse; creatively stating your truth; poetry flows from the right-brain.

Poison Often an inner danger; dangerous substances; vindictive intentions; 'swallowing' other people's philosophies without considering whether they're appropriate for you, as in 'one man's meat is another man's poison'.

Poker To gamble; a bluff; stoic, unemotional, as in 'poker-faced'.

Police Authority figures; keeping the peace; protection and care; if negative, corruption and bribery; or may be a police officer you know in waking life.

Politician Leader; ideals; corruption; bending to the whims of the majority.

Pond Your emotions, usually still and calm although confined; ripples are the dramas in your waking life. See also **Swimming pool**.

Pony Galloping through life; childhood dreams; fun. See also **Horse**.

Poo See **Defecate, Faeces, Nappy, Shit.**

Pool Join resources, as in 'car-pool', 'typing pool. See also **Swimming pool**.

Poor Less than; 'poor in spirit'; sympathy, as in 'poor thing'. See also **Poverty**.

Pope Spiritual leader; religious leader; Higher Self.

Port Safety; emotional security as 'any port in a storm'; a suitcase; a good wine.

Postman Messenger; someone bringing you news; literally, a letter.

Posture See **Stature.**

Pot Marijuana; a vessel or container; a prize; 'go to pot;—ruined.

Pottery Forming your own ideas, beliefs and concepts; or a vessel containing your gifts, emotions or purpose.

Poverty Poor outlook; poorly thought of; unaware of riches within.

Pregnant Full of ideas; ripe; may be literal; pregnant with possibilities.

Premonition A dream come true; usually more vivid; happen in threes or be accompanied by strong feelings.

President Authority figure.

Price 'Price-tag'. See also **Cost, Money**.

Priest Spiritual teacher; religion; confessing your wrongs; spiritual pursuits; Higher Self.

Prince The idealised male partner; your desires; your own princely qualities. See also **Masculine**.

Princess The idealised female partner; your desires; your own princess-like qualities. See also **Feminine**.

Prison Trapped in your life; feeling confined; limited; taking the consequences of your actions; biding time behind bars.

Prisoner The part of you, or someone else, that feels trapped or confined; waiting to escape your current circumstances; paying for your actions. See also **Criminal**.

Prize Something precious; congratulations; something or someone to be won or gained.

Prophet Higher Self; the spiritual part of yourself; great wisdom, direct knowledge. See also **Guru**.

Prostitute Feeling taken advantage of, especially sexually; giving power to another; 'cheap' sex; living out fears and fantasies in your dreams.

Psychiatrist Higher Self; the analytical, understanding, problem-solving part of yourself; may be a psychologist or psychiatrist you know in waking life.

Pub A pub, club or bar is a cultural symbol in Anglo-Saxon society, relating to social life, male bonding rituals, relaxing after work, Australian mateship, letting go of control or generally being raucous. See also **Bar, Beer**.

Punch As in 'Punch and Judy'. See also **Fight**.

Puppet In someone else's control. Who is pulling your strings?

Purple The self, the being, I am; 'royal purple'; the 'purple passions' of wild romance.

Purse Usually related to money issues; someone's purse strings.

Puzzle Something to be solved, worked out; puzzled, curious, uncertain, unclear.

Pyjamas Symbol of sleep and rest; sickness; relaxation; unconcerned about image; true self.

Pyramid An initiation; can be a past life-time in Egypt; a mystery.

Python Constricting; strangling; constraining; being 'squeezed'.

Qq... *Question 'why', however eccentric or everyday the message seems. Welcome both the inspirational and the mundane. Be open-minded—ever quizzical—open-hearted and open-armed, for closed you cannot receive.*

Quagmire A quaking bog; very dangerous ground; stuck in some issue.

Quarantine Period of isolation associated with illness of separation.

Quarrel Conflict; argument; drama or disagreement with self or another; usually relates to your present problems.

Queen Queen of your world; authority figure; goddess; pompous attitudes; ruler; a female cat; acting on someone else's behalf; a male homosexual.

Queer Peculiar or odd; a male homosexual.

Quest Your life's quest or search for something of great value or meaning.

Question Something unanswered or unexplained in your life.

Queue As in 'join the queue'—wait in line, waiting your turn.

Quicksand An unsure footing; circumstances are threatening to pull you down.

Quilt A cover-up; nurturing. See also **Blanket**.

Quip Sarcastic remarks; clever sayings; attention-getting dream messages.

Quiz Examine by questioning; exam fears; what do you think you don't know?

Quota Quantity of goods or services, as in 'meet the quota'.

Rr... Resurrect the child in you. Retrace the trials and errors that taught you to distrust your inner voice. Remember your ideals and the potential that you saw in yourself; and you will always see yourself renewed—as your Dream Teacher does.

Rabbi A teacher; religious leader; authority figure; spiritual guidance.

Rabbit Family connections; 'breed like rabbits'; a part of your natural instincts, which you bury from view; burrowing into the subconscious mind; timid; harmless.

Race Competitiveness, as 'in the race'; ambition, something you're racing to achieve; 'race against time'—time limitations.

Radio Ability to 'tune in' to your self or others; listen to or hear something.

Rage Often suppressed in waking life—will surface in dreams.

Rags Poverty;' down and out; 'rags to riches'; despair, emotional poverty.

Rails Support; 'off the rails'—out of control.

Railway station See **Station** and **Train**.

Rain Life-sustaining force; released emotions, sadness.

Rainbow Uplifting experience; a symbol of hope; your life's dreams; the unknown, 'over the rainbow'; spirituality; another reality; completions and new beginnings; the joy and cleansing that comes after an emotional storm; fulfilment, as in 'pot of gold at the end of the rainbow'.

Rake 'Rake in'; 'rake up'; to gather something; is it hard or easy?

Rape Being taken advantage of, anything done to you against your will; playing out a sexual fear or fantasy in your dreams; sexual issues, either 'victim'; one being raped, or as aggressor, 'the rapist'; using something beyond it's capacity to regenerate, as in 'raping the fields'; watch both your behaviour and your companions.

Rare Something special or unique; a gift from within or a special gift from your Higher Self.

Rat Someone you can't trust; malevolent intentions, motives; disease; gnawing thoughts or feelings.

Razor Innovative thought, as 'the cutting edge'; tool for trimming away unwanted thoughts or behaviours; clarity and a quick mind, as in 'razor sharp'.

Reaching Grasping for something; often something out of reach or something that you can't see; a level of anxiety or desperation, to reach unrealistic goals; can also 'be in easy reach'—closer than you think.

Reading Seeking knowledge, understanding or wisdom. See also **Library**.

Rear The past; what's behind you; 'at the rear'—last.

Recipe Something that works when you follow the steps.

Records Akashic records; Karma; unconscious guilt or shame.

Red Red is the colour of blood, passion, energy and aliveness; colour worn by Roman Catholic Cardinals.

Red-light area Sex for sale; a prostitute; buying or selling sex; the wild or taboo side of life; sleazy, sordid.

Reef Something dangerous hidden beneath the surface of your emotions; beware.

Refrigerator Source of nourishment; putting your feelings on ice; frigidity.

Relatives You may be visiting them in your astral body; on this plane or other planes of existence, if they are deceased; can be aspects of inherited beliefs or family patterns; genetic memory.

Religion Conventional spiritual pursuits.

Rent Hire from someone else; renting a house can symbolise adopting someone else's lifestyle.

Repair Something in your life needs fixing; making amends for past wrongs.

Rescue In need of help; salvage; what is it about you that needs rescuing?

Restaurant Issues around hunger, nourishment; friendship; socialising.

Reunion Get together with friends or relatives on a higher plane; review the past; take stock; preparing for a future step by 'touching base', going 'home' first.

Revelation A spiritual revelation; a teaching dream; an inkling of your life purpose in a dream; a universal truth revealed.

Revenge Seeking vengeance; a response to an offence or injustice; too much keeps you tied to the cycles of Karma.

Ride On an animal a sign of natural joy and attunement to nature; 'taken for a ride', duped or deceived.

Right As the 'correct' action or answer; being 'all right' or perfect; right side of the body (masculine, aggression, logic, masculine issues, the men in your life) connected to the left-brain.

Right-brain Connected to the left side of the body and the feminine focus, its functions are: colour; musical; metaphorical; existential; receptive; continuous; rhythmic; intuitive; focused in spatial time; integration; and a holistic awareness.

Ring Eternal; a love bond between two people. See also **Circle**, **Jewellery**.

Ringing Bell or alarm, wake up to something you avoid dealing with in life.

Rip See **Current, Tear**.

Rising Reaching a higher perspective; higher plane of existence; as 'rising water'—emotions rising to the surface; climbing the career ladder.

River River of life; source of emotional flow; perhaps an emotional barrier to cross.

Road What's ahead or your life's path, is it smooth or bumpy? See also **Crossroads, Journey, Path**.

Robot Mechanical, without emotion.

Rock An obstacle, as in 'a rocky path'; stability as in 'build on the rock'; stones, as in diamonds—wealth, security; hard or difficult, cold or 'stony'.

Rocket Soaring to infinite heights; exploring universal space.

Rod Will-power; strength. See also **Staff**.

Rodent See **Mouse, Rat**.

Roof Protection; conscious thought; higher perspective; reaching a limit. See also **Ceiling**.

Room An aspect of yourself. See individual rooms.

Rooster 'Crowing' about achievements; pride, as in 'strutting your stuff'; dawn, an awakening.

Roots As in 'origins'; inner strength and stability; what's hidden beneath the surface; grounded, earthy.

Rope Connection; 'rope in' ideas; bound or restricted; lifeline. See also **String**.

Rosary Repentance; a spiritual lesson; forgive yourself.

Rose Symbol of love and romance. See also **Flowers**.

Rubbish Garbage; worthless nonsense; waste and debris, clean up your life now!

Rubies Believed to harness the creative powers of the sun; has also been said to represent Adam's 'red flesh'; Leo birthstone.

Rudder How you steer through your life and especially your emotions.

Ruins What remains of something from your past; despair over something you believe is ruined.

Running Moving too fast through life; escaping from a problem or yourself; what are you running from?; where are you running to? See also **Race**.

Rust Something is corroding or breaking down in your life; something decaying or something in need of attention; or as in 'I'm a bit rusty'.

Rustic setting A need for peace and quiet; may indicate your personal sanctuary.

Rut Trapped in a 'rut', which can be a relationship or a job, or you can't find a solution. For things to change first you must change. See also **Ditch, Valley**.

Ss... *Scintillating, symbols of the soul's creativity will surge forth in dreams as shrewd reminders of the constancy of your self-expression. Serious or satirical, sexy or studious, strut your stuff!*

Saboteur One who sabotages someone or something; beware, it may be you.

Sacred Something of great value; divine knowledge or awareness.

Sacrifice Giving up something; an offering; 'self-sacrificing'; feeling as though your needs are not being met; what is being sacrificed in your life? See also **Martyr**.

Saddle You and your instincts, as in 'at home in the saddle'; a burden, as in 'being saddled' with something.

Sadism Pleasure from inflicting or watching cruelty.

Safari A tour to observe animals in the wild. See also **Trek**.

Sail Sailing through life, as the wind blows; how you symbolically move through your emotions.

Sailor Emotional courage; adventure and travel.

Saint Your Guardian Angel. Higher Self manifesting in your dreams.

Salad Health and vitality, energy and aliveness; may be as dietary advice.

Salary What you're worth; payment for your efforts; energy exchange. See also **Wage**.

Salesman The part of you who 'sells' yourself to others, putting your best foot forward; 'a foot in the door'; this quality in someone else; may be a salesperson you know in waking life.

Salt Valuable substance; seasoning; something tasty that brings out the flavour of other things; 'salt of the earth', an earthy type.

Sanctuary A peaceful place in your life; an inner sanctuary; a feeling of peace; a place of protection from the events around you, can be a sacred place or 'inner space'.

Sand Shifting emotions, as in 'shifting sands'; a measure of time, as in 'sands of time'; no foundations. See also **Beach, Desert, Quicksand**.

Sandals See **Shoes**.

Sapphire Most commonly associated with fate; hope and happiness; in Hinduism it represents fertility, after the goddess Lalita; Buddhists used its magical powers to 'sleepwalk', astrologers associate it with the enlightened.

Saw Hacking through an issue in life.

Scales Weighing things up; seeking either balance or justice.

Scar A past hurt now healed; or an old wound that needs healing.

School Learning a life lesson, as in 'the school of life'; spiritual instruction, as in ancient Mystery Schools; can also be a time warp back to your childhood; the school you attend in waking life.

Scientist The questioning, analytical left-brain part of yourself or someone else; may literally be a scientist from your waking life.

Scissors Cutting through to the truth; a division; cutting ties or energy that bind you to others; cut off.

Scorpion A dangerous person, able to 'sting' you with their comments; this aspect of your own nature; or someone with a Scorpio horoscope.

Scream Fear or rage; the emotional release of a scream aids emotional health.

Screen Something hidden, as in 'as smokescreen'.

Scrotum Sexual energy; courage, as in 'balls'.

Sea See **Ocean**.

Seagull High-flying; expansiveness of spirit; self-esteem and inner knowing.

Seal 'Seal of approval'; closing an issue, as in 'signed, sealed and delivered'.

Seam Where things are sown or bound together; 'coming apart at the seams'.

Seasons

    Spring Renewed life; new beginnings; eternal youth; joy.

    Summer Warmth; a harvesting of fruits.

Autumn Release of the old; falling away of the past; review.

Winter Hibernation; going within ; completion.

Seatbelt A need for protection on life's journey; prevention or restraint.

Secret Something not revealed to yourself or to others; can be a hidden truth.

Secretary Organisation; efficiency; helpfulness; may be a secretary from your waking life.

Sedative Suppressing an issue; escaping the reality of your true feelings; dampening the impact of some emotional drama; not wanting to feel something repressed or suppressed emotions or sedated energy and aliveness.

Seed The beginning of something; 'a seed of doubt'; an idea; the raw material of life.

Seesaw Moving between two options; up and down; changing your mind.

Semen Released seed during sex; procreation; potency may indicate sexual trauma if recurring in dreams or nightmares.

Semi-trailer A big load to bear; feeling overloaded or cumbersome.

Sentry A guard on guard; guarding secrets; watching someone or something.

Servant As a servant, bowing to someone else's wishes; putting someone else before yourself; to serve, be of service; who are you serving, or who do you expect to serve you? See also **Slave**.

Seven A mystical number of truth; the seventh day is a day of rest. It symbolises humanity touching the spiritual realm to receive wisdom.

Sew Creating something in your life; mending a tear or rip, making a difference; update your image. See also **Clothes**.

Sewage Waste products; something unused; something believed to be 'dirty'.

Sex Living out your fantasies in dreams; lack of sex in your waking life; unity; bonding; harmony between male and female parts of yourself; passionate expressions of love.

Shadow Hidden or shadow-self; something or someone that follows in your wake; a symbol of your fears; the shadowy, darker or taboo side of life.

Shallow Shallow or safer emotions; fear of intimacy, afraid to go deeper. See also **Ocean**.

Shampoo Spiritual cleaning revitalising your personal power. See also **Hair**.

Shark Someone you don't trust; a predator; beware of 'sharks', or being taken advantage of, ending up as shark-bait.

Shave Trimming away unwanted behaviours and burdens; revealing the real you; a lucky escape, as in 'a close shave'.

Sheep Following the 'herd'; lack of individuality; timidly bleating out your concerns.

Sheets Sleeping; sex; rest; covering something up in your life.

Shelf Storing something for the future, as on a 'mental shelf'.

Shells Ancient values; natural beauty; a protective covering.

Shelter Protection; safety; respite from conflict or storm.

Shelves Layers of understanding; a 'mental shelf' See also **Cupboard**.

Shield Protection against attack; a psychic shield.

Ship See **Boat**.

Shit Term of abuse, as in 'You shit!'; 'shit-faced'—drunk. See also **Defecate, Faeces**.

Shoes Personal direction; relate to how you walk through life.

Shooting Star Enhanced potential; personal creativity and power; 'guiding star'.

Shop, shopping To shop; shopping around; looking for something; what is it you need?

Shoulder 'Shoulder the burden' of genetic memory and 'learned' patterns.

Shot The Victim, penetrated, in grave danger; 'to give it your best shot' or hit the target.

Shower Cleansing; refreshing; spiritual cleansing.

Sick What are you sick and tired of in your life? See **Disease**.

Sign A signal or message for you.

Silk Sensual; richness; feeling good, smooth.

Silver Metal of the moon; feminine receptive power; conduit for bio-electrical energy; as a colour, the pure light of illumination.

Singing Breathing; chanting; expressing emotion wholeheartedly, exultation; especially chanting the name of God as an Eastern spiritual discipline.

Sink Cleaning up after yourself; cleansing. See also **Drain**.

Sinking Sinking into depression; sinking into your emotions; 'sink or swim'; into the subconscious; an area of your life that's going downhill.

Siren Alarm; pay attention.

Sister Literally, your sister; sisterhood; friendship; in service as a nun.

Six Personal responsibility and service; six represents relationships.

Skate Moving smoothly through life; a risk, as in 'skating on thin ice'.

Skeleton The bone level of an issue; outline of a project or a proposal; unprotected; lack of emotions; spirit-less or dead; symbol of fear. See also **Bones, Death**.

Ski Balance and speed; are you 'in control' or 'out of control'.

Skin Layer of protection; superficial, as in 'skin-deep'.

Sky No limits, as in 'the sky is the limit'; big goals; spiritual awareness; an expansive nature.

Slap Disapproval; an insult, as in 'a slap in the face'.

Slave In someone else's keeping; 'sex-slave'; a past life; slave to an addiction; who or what is your master? See also **Servant**.

Sleep, Sleeping Not aware of something; unaware of some problem or issue; accessing other levels of consciousness.

Slip As in 'Freudian slip'—the truth accidentally slips out.

Slippers 'Dancing' slippers; 'bedroom' slippers—walking through life in a relaxed way; lack of awareness; sickness or illness.

Slipping Making a mistake, as in 'as a slip-up'. See also **Falling**.

Smoke Sign of trouble, as in 'where there's smoke, there's fire'; 'smoky', as in passionate; lack of clarity; putting up a false image, as in 'a smokescreen.' See also **Cigarettes, Fire**.

Snail Crawling through life 'at a snail's pace'—slow progression in life.

Snake Eternal life; reincarnation; immortality; wisdom; masculine creative power; sex and sexuality; energy; venomous feelings; evil; Kundalini energy of aliveness; phallus; fertility; depends on how your personally feel about snakes.

Sneeze Natural way to charge up your aura or bio-electrical energy field.

Snitch To tell on, as in 'snitched to the teacher'; divided loyalties.

Snout As in police 'snout' or informant.

Snow Frozen emotions or situations; to be 'frozen out' or given 'the cold shoulder'; 'a snow job'—cover-up; depending on feeling in dream, can mean clarity or cleansing; the drug cocaine which suppresses fatigue and fear.

Soap Cleansing; purifying; washing away a problem. See also **Bathroom, Laundry**.

Soldier Authority figure; protector; brave warrior; national service.

Solicitor Laying down the law; the part of yourself that protects and defends you; may be a solicitor you actually know.

Somersaults Expression of joy; leaping over a problem; turned upside-down about a decision you have made; making an about-face.

Son May, literally, be your son; the young boy that is a part of you; if female, your animus.

Song Personal relevance, depending on context and lyrics. See also **Music, Singing**.

South The forehead, the front brain and pituitary gland, the third eye.

Spear Attack; defence. See also **Weapon, Dart, Arrow**.

Spectacles Dim view; can't see clearly; what don't you want to see?

Speed Moving too fast through life or not fast enough; eager to reach your destination.

Sperm Procreation; new beginnings; sex; potency; competing for a goal. See also **Semen**.

Spider Unconscious fears; danger; venomous; depends on your feelings about spiders; a symbol of feminine power, as in attracting into a web'; can indicate a change of destiny; a 'rock spider'—for child molester.

Spider's web The web of destiny or life; a trap; falling prey to someone; someone has power over you; 'what a tangled web we weave, when first we practice to deceive'; lies as in 'web of deceit'.

Spine Support; courage, as in 'backbone'; 'spineless coward.'.

Spiral RNA, DNA helix; the image of personal evolution; as a spiral staircase; moving upward, as the world turns.

Splinter Penetration; break; irritation; fragment of an issue which is not yet resolved.

Sponge Taking advantage as in 'a sponger'; are you one or the victim of one?

Spoon Implement for nourishment and nurturing; assistance, as in 'being spoonfed' or babied.

Sport Treats life like a game; competitiveness; don't be unreasonable, be a goodsport' about it.

Spy Prying into someone's secrets.

Square Balanced as in 'a square meal'; 'square' not 'hip'; organised, established, establishment.

Staff Strength; mainstay; suit of clubs or suit of staffs in Tarot cards; spiritual knowledge, wisdom.

Stage The stage of life; image or personal appearance; stage of an issue; a difficult stage; 'on stage'; self-expression.

Stain Something has left its mark.

Stairs Steps to be taken to accomplish something; if going up—towards spirit and higher ideals; if down—into the subconscious. See also **Spiral**.

Stamp Stamp of approval or ownership.

Stars Reaching for great heights in life; evolving; insight; guidance; success; to follow your guiding star.

Starving An emotional need or hunger.

Station Embarking on your journey; changing directions; new levels; taking a pause in your life's journey. See also **Train**.

Stature Height; posture or position in life; lifeless.

Steal Take something from another. Why can't you meet your own needs without diminishing another's supply? Fear of not enough.

Steel Strength; protection, reinforced; 'nerves of steel'.

Steep Difficult obstacle; point of great learning.

Steering wheel Steering your self or your way through life.

Steps Steps to be taken up or down.

Stingray 'Stinging' emotions or issues; 'stung'—taken advantage of.

Stomach Centre of power and fear; what can't you stomach?

Stone Immovable; impassable; emotion-less, as in 'stony'; solid support.

Stoned Escaping from reality, either drunk or drugged.

Store The storeroom of your mind. See also **Shop**.

Storm Stormy emotions; strife or trouble; 'to weather the storm'.

Stove See **Baking, Oven**.

Stranger An unknown aspect of yourself; may represent someone you know or will know in the future.

Strangle See **Choking**.

Straw As 'the short straw' or 'the last straw'; drinking straw.

Stream See **River**.

Street An aspect of your life's path.

Streetlights Illuminating your life's journey; able to see where you're heading.

String Connections; attachments to others; 'string someone along'—uncommitted. See also **Rope**.

Struggle Conflict; inner struggle to get into or out of something.

Student The part of you that craves knowledge, and is a perpetual student of life; may, literally, be a student you know.

Study Something to be learned.

Submarine Investigating your deepest emotions; deep subconscious; feeling submerged in your emotions.

Success What you do with a good opportunity in life.

Suck On the breast, nurturing; time warp to childhood; being 'sucked in to something'; something you don't like or want to do, as in 'this sucks'; sexual as in 'suck off'. See also **Breast**.

Suffocating Feeling suffocated or smothered by someone. See also **Choking**.

Suicide Not wanting to continue on your chosen path; giving up; death or a 'killing off' of an old part of the self; a dangerous path in life, as in 'slow suicide'.

Suitcase See **Luggage**.

Sun Guiding light; purification; source of highest energy; Higher Self; a light of awareness.

Sunflower A large bright golden flower with edible seeds. Life-giving symbol of summer, joy and plenty.

Sunglasses Trendy self-image; a dim view of things; What are you hiding behind?

Supermarket See **Shop**.

Surf, surfing The waves of your emotions; riding the waves of your emotions.

Swamp Swamped by emotions; confusion and/or fear; overwhelmed.

Swan A graceful person; spiritual grace; emotional evolution; great beauty.

Sweat In sleep can signify the result of a difficult job; a physical cleansing; a release of fear.

Sweeping Sweeping out unwanted habits or areas of your life that need cleaning up.

Sweets A special treat; enjoyment of life.

Swim 'Sink or swim'; ready to dive in; at one with your subconscious or your emotions.

Swimming pool Contained emotions; safer emotions, depending on dream context. See also **Pond**.

Switch Making a change; bringing awareness into your life, as in 'switching on the light'; new goals, new discipline.

Sword Gallantry; honour; attack and defence; cutting through the illusion to the truth; the suit of swords in Tarot cards or the suit of Spades in playing cards. See also **Weapon**.

Syringe Need an injection of something in your life; penetration; facing the consequences of your actions, as in 'take your medicine'; healing; addiction. See also **Needle, Injection**.

Tt... *Teamwork brings about inspirational results and your Dream Teacher can't work effectively without your co-operation. It's just as well that Dream Teachers are so persistent and truly patient.*

Table Issues around communication, sharing, eating and working; negotiation. See also **Dining room, Kitchen.**

Tablet A stone tablet, or message from God. See also **Medicine, Pill.**

Tail The end of a problem; that which brings up the rear.

Tailbone See **Base, Coccyx.**

Tailor The person or part of yourself that enhances your image; 'tailor-made'.

Talmud Spiritual wisdom.

Tangled In a mess; confused; intricate webs or connections.

Tap Ability to turn emotions off and on, as in 'on tap'; listening in to other people's conversations and lives, as in 'to tap the phone'; a 'tap on the shoulder'—a warning.

Tapes Learned patterns from parents; parental disapproval issues.

Tapestry As in 'life's rich tapestry'; weaving your destiny.

Target Goal. See also **Bullseye.**

Tax Tithe to government, a percentage of one's income; 'taxed to the limit'; fair taxes; taxing of strength or resources.

Taxi Allowing someone else to take you through life; literally, a taxi.

Tea 'Tea-time'—taking a break; relaxing; friendship, sharing.

Teacher Authority figure; something you need to learn or can teach others.

Tear Something has been ripped apart in your life; a torn relationship.

Tears An emotional cleansing; a release of toxins; emotional healing.

Teeth Especially when you dream your teeth are falling out— wishy-washy, unable to make decisions; self-deception, lies and false pretences, as in 'lying through your teeth'—maybe you are too 'nice' to say what you truly feel. See also **Chew**.

Telephone Communication with others, often telepathy or telepathic information; a message from your Higher Self.

Television Receiver of messages; information; awareness of the issues of others; mass consciousness; or how to appear to yourself.

Temple Inner sanctuary; a spiritual 'space'; place of peace and beauty.

Ten The number of completion; a wholeness; unity.

Tent On the road; camping; roughing it; moving on.

Terrorists You or someone else is sabotaging something in your life; terror.

Test An advancement in some area of your life, depending on context. See also **Exam**.

Theatre Roles in life; role-playing; acting out; playing a part; theatrical or dramatic. See also **Arena, Movie, Play**.

Thief A spiritual or emotional thief, someone who takes our time, energy or 'space'. In some cases an actual thief.

Thin Emotionally starved; unprotected; a belief in scarcity.

Third eye Point between the eyebrows; the site of intuition and psychic power.

Thirty Three A master number that relates to both the universal and personal laws of Karma.

Thongs Walking very casually through life.

Thorn Something bothering you, demands attention, as in 'a thorn in the side'.

Three Represents the creativity and self-expression of the choices and commitments we make that ultimately mould our lives.

Throat Communication; self-expression; unable to express true feelings or to speak up for self.

Throne To 'enthrone', as in put on a pedestal; an ego trip.

Thumb See **Fingers**.

Thunder Voice of the gods; a much needed release of suppressed emotions, especially anger or rage; a psychic release; a natural warning of rain to follow.

Tidal wave Emotionally overwhelmed; waves of overpowering emotions.

Tide Ebb and flow of emotions associated with waxing and waning of the moon.

Tie Family ties; emotional bonds; shared experiences; establishment; 'old school tie'.

Tiger Sexuality; promiscuity; power; strength; feline qualities; sensuality.

Tired Exhaustion; tired of something or someone in your life; avoiding facing an emotional issue.

Toad Someone you don't respect, as in 'a toad'; or hidden ugliness.

Toes Our grip on life.
> **Big** The intellect—neck and head.
> **Second** The emotions.
> **Middle** Balance.
> **Fourth** Sexual.
> **Little** Fear.

Toilet Elimination; cleansing; physical, emotional, mental or spiritual release of old beliefs, fears or patterns.

Toilet paper No toilet paper in a dream indicates a normal situation where it's a public toilet, or difficulty achieving elimination or release of unhealthy patterns.

Tongue Self-expression; the way you communicate; harsh comments, as in 'a sharp tongue'; 'silver tongue'—smooth talker; if tongue is cut off, reflects an inability to communicate.

Tools Anything to assist you in life—skills, objects, people.

Toothbrush 'Cleaning your mouth out'; a need for 'fresh' words.

Tooting Blowing own horn; wake up; warning others of danger.

Top Top position; a goal; 'top form'—peak condition.

Topaz Believed to have a cheering effect. Mental stimulation, helps recuperation. Some have attributed it to helping cure insomnia.

Torch Illuminating your life's path; awareness shared.

Tortoise Moving slowly but surely through life; long life. See also **Turtle**.

Torture Feeling tortured or victimised in life; torturing others.

Tour Pleasant or unpleasant company on your life's path. See also **Guide.**.

Tourmaline A conductor of power or electricity; aids channelling.

Tower The tower of your accomplishments; an ancient or established aspect of yourself; an overview or higher perspective; may be a warning of inner change.

Toy Something to amuse yourself with; to 'toy' or 'toying'—play with.

Track Following a set path in your life.

Traffic An awareness of where other people are on their life's journey.

Traffic lights An indicator of your ease of movement through life.

Trail Following a set path in your life.

Train Moving through life on conventional or set 'rails'.

Transport How you move through life. See individual means of transport, **Bicycle, Car**, etc.

Trap Feeling trapped; be aware of hidden traps in your life.

Trash Garbage; destroy as in to 'trash it'; 'trashy'—cheap.

Travel Moving into new areas of your life; may actually be astral travelling.

Treadmill Constant movement, going nowhere; stuck in a situaion. See also **Rut**.

Treasure A material goal; richness; look for treasure; treasure yourself. Gifts from the gods, inner wealth.

Trees Essentially you, or an influential person you know or will know; personal growth (green and full—abundance; barren and bare—a need to look within) type ('weeping willow'—wispy; 'solid as an oak'; graceful poplars; winding wistaria); Palm trees in tropical heat; trees for providing food or shelter; fruitful and productive; family tree.

Trek Embarking on an inner journey in life. See also **Quest, Safari**.

Triangle Can be symbolic of a love triangle; esoteric wisdom; trinity.

Tribe People with the same values and beliefs as you; family; bonding.

Trough See **Ditch, Rut, Valley.**

Truck Big potential; 'trucking' through life at a comfortable pace; if negative, a heavy load to carry.

Trunk Something out of view; the subconscious. See also **Container.**

Tumour Something growing out of control in your life, growing very fast; something which needs to be surgically removed from your life.

Tunnel Moving through birth experience; Karma, birth, death and rebirth; can be closed-mindedness, as in 'tunnel-vision'; tunnelling through the subconscious and unconscious; finding your way through an obstacle.

Turquoise Represents luck and money. In ancient Persia and Turkey it was used to protect from head injury, lung and respiratory system infection.

Turtle Someone at ease emotionally.

Twenty-two A master number; spiritual; mystical aid to conscious co-operation.

Two An expression of life energy through duality; interaction or cooperation between opposites; represents harmony and co-operation; partnerships.

Typewriter Take note of your thoughts; communicate; actual work.

Tyre Obese, as in 'spare tyre'; a play on words as 'to tire'; an indication of how you travel through life, as in 'flat tyre'; unbalanced, delayed; no movement.

Uu... *Unite every dream symbol. Only when they are all together, united and whole, can we see how each piece makes the picture complete. Then you can be utterly dignified, charming, effervescent and continually nurturing of yourself.*

Umbrella If open, protection from or by something; supporting as in 'umbrella company'; overview; if closed, unaware of protection; emotional safety.

Underground Buried in the subconscious; subterranean, ancient or secret.

Underwear Sexual persona.

Undressing Showing true self; if negative, unable to hide or have any privacy.

Unemployed Lacking in personal direction; if you are unemployed in waking life, your dream may be 'playing out' your fears—search for clues in your dream as to your new directions and advice for the appropriate action for you at this time.

Uniform Traditional; someone else's ideals; uniform, established rigid forms.

University Lessons and learning; free-thinking, as in 'university of life'.

Unprepared Resolving a fear in your dream time; feeling unready for something; afraid of confrontation; not prepared to make a commitment.

Up 'On the up and up'—higher and higher; moving to greater awareness or understanding in your life.

Upstairs Thinking; right direction; higher levels of consciousness.

Urinate Letting go of stale thoughts and old patterns; anger; as in 'pissed off'; disrespect, as in 'pissing on' someone, a cleansing and releasing of something.

Urine Old thoughts and patterns; the effluent of your actions.

Urn Reincarnation; receptical for ashes for the dead.

Vv... Victory is the acceptance of each and every dream visitor. It is a sign of your valour, your determination, your vision and your capability to overcome even your greatest fears.

Vacation See **Holiday**.

Vagina Sexual issues; body issues; potency; receptivity; especially as an unconscious birth memory. See also **Femininity**, **Genitals**.

Valley Feeling low or down, as in 'high mountain, low valley'.

Vampire Someone who 'sucks others dry', draining their thoughts and their energy, aliveness, life force or soul. See also **Bat**.

Vandalism Disrespect for what belongs to someone else; making a clever, witty, personal or idealistic statement; to destroy, with or without an awareness of value.

Vase Symbol of the feminine; container of flowers given in love.

Vegetable Nutrition; healthy; can be a message to eat or not eat a particular food.

Vehicle An expression of how you move through life. See individual modes of transport, **Bicycle**, **Car**, etc.

Veil Something concealed; secret or hidden; not seeing clearly; may be a bridal veil.

Venom Hostile; venomous thoughts and actions; vindictiveness; defence.

Vessel Symbol of the feminine as vase or pot. See also **Boat**.

Vet A part of you or someone else responsible for the health of your animal instincts; an expert at handling your animal nature; 'to vet'—examine.

Victim Feeling powerless; a victim to another's power. Turn and face your attacker. Find your inner strength and power. Once you can do this in your dream time, you can also bring it to your waking life.

Vine As in 'clinging'; bonding; a connection; 'fruit on the vine'—abundance.

Violet Spiritual attainment, as one with all living things.

Virgin Pure; fresh; untouched or untried; goodness; innocence; naivety; may relate to unconscious traumatic sexual issues depending on other clues.

Volcano Emotional explosions as volcanic eruptions.

Vomit Rejecting something that may not be as good for you as first thought. Release what is making you sick or what you are sick of feeling about yourself; old attitudes and beliefs need release now.

Vulture Something circling above, waits for death; release of old beliefs.

Ww... Wisdom often comes in whimsical forms. It is sociable, impulsive, free, exploratory, cloaked as a prince or a frog. It can be found in a pit of snakes or on a roller-coaster. Especially if it comes in a dream.

Wage Amount paid for work done. See also **Money, Salary**.

Waiter Pandering to your needs for nurturing and nourishment; expecting to be served; a service to others; may be a waiter you know in waking life.

Waitress As **Waiter**; any female who 'waits' on you, cares for or serves you.

Walk As you walk through life; more involved and detailed view; can relate to who is walking with you.

Wallaby See **Kangaroo**.

Wallet Wealth; possessions; your identity or position. See also **Money**.

Walls As barriers, obstacles to be overcome; as protection, 'walled in'; private.

Wand Making things happen, as in 'magic wand'; acting on inspiration; your creative power; personal direction; the suit of Clubs in playing cards; the suit of Staffs, Rods or Wands in Tarot cards as a strengthening inspiration; ideals; thoughts, beliefs or spiritual disciplines.

War Conflict on any level; personal, as in 'inner battle'; war between the sexes, relationship dramas; as war against crime, community battles; global, as war against disease; actual wars happening in the world will feature in our dreams and may take place in the city or even on the street where we live; especially detailed media coverage of any battle will often appear in our dreams, allowing us to 'feel with' or empathise with others; can also indicate past-life or genetic memory.

Wardrobe Can indicate image, as in a 'new wardrobe'; a place to hide; a favourite hiding place for monsters in children's dreams. See also **Clothes**.

Warehouse Where you store needed stock or aspects of yourself.

Warlock Dark deceiving black wizard or sorcerer. See also **Magician**.

Warm Friendliness; lack of fear; relaxed; getting close to the truth, as in 'you're getting warm.

Warrior The veteran or soldier within you. If female, your animus. See also **War**.

Warts Manifestations of self-loathing.

Washing Cleaning out the old; renewing; refreshing. See also **Bathroom**.

Wasp Nasty or 'stinging' comments; 'WASP' (White Anglo-Saxon Protestant). See also **Bee**.

Watch Time factor involved; 'watch' out for something, especially your personal timing; it may be later than you think.

Water Source of life; a life-sustaining force; pure when clear and running, muddy indicates lack of clarity or confusion shame or guilt; as baptism, a connection to the Holy Spirit; a symbol of the emotions as the element, water; calm or turbulent emotions.

Waterfall Overflow or release of emotions; a powerful emotional cleansing.

Waves Turbulent emotions; the ebbs and troughs in life; unless you are a sailor or a surfer, in which case they will have many different distinctions in your life. See also **Tidal wave**.

Weak Feeling powerless; helpless; drained of energy and aliveness.

Weather An emotional scale—stormy or calm, cold or warm.

Weapon Any tool used by you or against you for attack or self-defence can indicate an inner battle or a need to empower yourself. See also **Gun, Harpoon, Knife**.

Weave To form a thread into fabric, hence weaving the fabric of one's life; creating your own destiny; weaving your opportunities; creative power. See also **Illusion, Tapestry**.

Web Woven by the self, as in 'a web of intrigue'; a trap; See also **Spiders web**.

Wedding Sometimes a prophetic dream if you are planning a wedding in your waking life; may be fantasy or wish-fulfilment; a celebration of unity; a bonding. See also Marriage.

Weed A sign of neglect; can be choking good aspects of life or good growth; something unwanted, possibly out of control.

Well The well of emotions; drink at the well to satisfy a thirst; a symbol of wealth in barren areas; or 'well-being'.

Werewolf Powerful symbol of bestial transformation; wildness; fear; aggression.

West Is the right-brain—the intuitive, rhythmic, holistic and spatial time.

Whale Keeper of ancient wisdom; a big opportunity, as in 'a whale of an idea'; powerful symbol of intuitive perception.

Wheel Wheel of Karma—wheel of fortune; the cycles of life. See also **Illusion, Weave**.

Whip Discipline; sexual fantasies played out in dreams; to whip something up, or create something.

Whiskers As in 'quivering with' ..., sensitivity to or awareness of what's around you.

Whisper Afraid to speak your truth; sensitivity to the reactions of others.

White Reflects all colours; a symbol of purity; the colour worn by the Pope.

Whore To 'go whoring' or seeking sex; to sell yourself. See also **Prostitute**.

Wife May, quite literally, be your wife; could also be the 'wife-like' aspect of yourself. What qualities do you attribute to a 'wife'; how do these apply to you?

Will Desire; wish; intention; a written will as in 'last testament'; a human faculty, as in in 'free will'; your constant power of choice.

Win A celebration as in 'win a race or trophy'; win a contract, be a winner.

Wind Essence of the element air; a change, as in 'blow away the cobwebs', or 'a breath of fresh air'.

Window A view of the world; a 'window of opportunity' opens; or a particular time; eyes are said to be the windows of the soul.

Wine Social, as in 'to wine and dine'; as Holy Communion. See **Alcohol**.

Wings Angelic freedom; setting free; a desire to soar; need for expansion.

Witch Female wizard, sorceress or magician; wise use of creative power; if evil, then a manifestation of your fears; a woman your fear; someone whose intentions and skills you don't trust.

Wizard Masculine creative power; a male witch; someone talented, or who can make things work, as in 'a wizard at what they do'.

Wolf As in 'the wolf at the door'; an imminent threat or physical fear; can be a symbol of wild instincts; outrageous flirt. See also **Dingo, Werewolf**.

Woman Feminine qualities within you; a woman you know in waking life; if male, it may be your anima.

Womb Protection; safety; a time warp back as far as your conception.

Wombat Sexual insensitivity; as in the saying 'eats, roots and leaves'; stupid; cuddly and innocuous.

Wood Inspired by life; stubborn; unbending.

Wooden Lifeless; impermanent; natural.

Wool To fool or be fooled, as in 'pull the wool over someone's eyes'. See also **Warm, Weave**.

Work Work to be done, either with someone, or work on something.

Worm Earthy, beneath the surface.

Wound Spiritual or emotional; a hurt. See also **Injury**.

Wreck Things have fallen apart; something unsuccessful; feeling or looking 'like a wreck'; an unexplored ancient part of yourself or a past life.

Wrestle A battle with self or a problem; wrestle with emotions; wrestle with life or a struggle.

Write To communicate.

Writing Messages; self-expression; communication.

$Xx...$ *X-rays of your subconscious and mind develop as dreams. If you don't examine them, how will you know what is broken or cracked or why you experience such terrible, nagging internal pain.*

X A symbol of something that is wrong; it can indicate where something is, as in 'X marks the spot'.

X-ray Seeing into someone, or into a part of yourself; seeing beyond the outer appearance of something or someone.

Yy... Yes, *there is a secret, mystical, intuitive part of yourself. Yes, there are universal concepts that science has still to explain. Yes, there is a much vaster part of you. Thank God for dreams that tell 'Y'.*

Yard See **Backyard, Garden**.

Yawn A way humans have of 'changing gear'. Yawning relaxes the face, jaw and scalp. To suppress a yawn is a wasted opportunity to relax and release stress. We often yawn when we are mentally overloaded or have misunderstood something. Yawning is catching—once one person yawns, several others do as well.

Yell To call out for help, or cry out in joy; en emotional release.

Yellow Intelligence, wisdom and knowledge, concepts and beliefs, choice and decision; connected also with cowardice, as in 'You yellow-bellied coward!'

Yin, Yang An ancient oriental symbol of equal and exactly balanced opposites, the creative and the receptive energies, masculine and feminine energies.

Yoga Hindu meditation and practice designed to reunite the soul with Universal Spirit.

Yogi One who is a teacher or devotee of the practice of yoga.

Yoke As in 'yoked to a plough'; a restraining collar, hence 'the yoke of slavery'.

Yo Yo Toy or plaything; returning on a string.

Youth Renewal or regeneration of energy and aliveness; may be a time warp dream.

Zz... Zany, bizarre, weird! Is that what you think of your dreams? Well, you are right; because from the point of view of your Dream Teacher all of your unhealthy fears are zany, bizarre and weird.

Zap Send a bolt of energy or electricity, as in 'zapped by lightning'.

Zebra crossing A safety area.

Zero Nothing. See also **Circle**.

Zigzag Cutting sharply back and forth, as not in a straight line.

Zip Something waiting to be opened or closed.

Zircon Symbol of humility; it has properties that are in a constant state of change. Used in the Middle Ages to help cure wasting diseases.

Zombie Emotionally dead; unfeeling; unconscious or unaware; literally, a corpse brought to life by voodoo or witchcraft.

Zoo A chaos; your animal instincts; these instincts may not be free to express themselves for some reason.